Divine Healing

Divine Healing

Andrew
MURRAY

Ⓦ *Whitaker House*

Unless otherwise noted, Scripture quotations are taken from the *King James Version* (KJV) of the Bible.

Scripture quotations marked (NKJV) are taken from the *New King James Version*, © 1979, 1980, 1982 by Thomas Nelson, Inc. Used by permission. All rights reserved.

Editor's note: This book has been edited for the modern reader. Words, expressions, and sentence structure have been updated for clarity and readability.

DIVINE HEALING

ISBN: 0-88368-642-2
Printed in the United States of America
© 1982 by Whitaker House

Whitaker House
30 Hunt Valley Circle
New Kensington, PA 15068

Library of Congress Cataloging-in-Publication Data

Murray, Andrew, 1828–1917.
  Divine healing / by Andrew Murray.
      p. cm.
  ISBN 0-88368-642-2 (pbk.)
  1. Spiritual healing. I. Title.
  BT732.5 .M86 2000
  234'.131—dc21   00-011728

2 3 4 5 6 7 8 9 10 11 12 / 08 07 06 05 04 03 02 01

Contents

Preface

The publication of this work may be regarded as a testimony of my faith in divine healing. After being stopped for more than two years in the exercise of my ministry, I was healed by the mercy of God in answer to the prayer of those who see in Him *"the LORD that healeth thee"* (Exod. 15:26).

This healing, granted to faith, has been the source of rich spiritual blessing to me. I have clearly seen that the church possesses in Jesus, our divine Healer, an inestimable treasure, which she does not yet know how to appreciate. I have been convinced anew of what the Word of God teaches us in this matter, and of what the Lord expects of us. I am sure that if Christians learned to realize, in a practical sense, the presence of the Lord who heals in their everyday lives, their spiritual lives would thereby be developed and sanctified.

I can, therefore, no longer keep silent. This series of meditations is published to show, according to the Word of God, that *"the prayer of faith"* (James 5:15) is the means appointed by God for the cure of the sick. My purpose is to show that this truth is in perfect accord with Holy Scripture, and that the study of this truth is essential for everyone who desires to see the Lord manifest His power and His glory in the midst of His children.

—ANDREW MURRAY

One

Pardon and Healing

But that ye may know that the Son of man hath power on earth to forgive sins (then saith he to the sick of the palsy), Arise, take up thy bed, and go unto thine house.
—Matthew 9:6

Man is a combination of opposing natures; he is at the same time spirit and matter, heaven and earth, soul and body. For this reason, on one side he is the son of God, and on the other he is doomed to destruction because of the Fall. Sin in his soul and sickness in his body bear witness to the right that death has over him. It is this twofold nature that has been redeemed by divine grace. When the psalmist called upon all that was within him to bless the Lord for His benefits, he cried, *"Bless the Lord, O my soul...who forgiveth all thine iniquities; who healeth all thy diseases"* (Ps. 103:2–3). When Isaiah foretold the deliverance of his people, he added, *"The inhabitant shall not say, I am sick; the people that dwell therein shall be forgiven their iniquity"* (Isa. 33:24).

9

Divine Healing

This prediction was accomplished beyond all anticipation when Jesus the Redeemer came down to this earth. How numerous were the healings brought about by Him who had come to establish on earth the kingdom of heaven! By His own acts and afterward by the commands that He left for His disciples, He showed us clearly that the preaching of the Gospel and the healing of the sick went together in the salvation that He came to bring. Both are given as evidence of His mission as the Messiah: *"The blind receive their sight, and the lame walk...and the poor have the gospel preached to them"* (Matt. 11:5). Jesus, who took upon Himself the soul and body of man, delivers both in equal measure from the consequences of sin.

This truth is nowhere more evident or better demonstrated than in the healing of the paralytic. The Lord Jesus began by saying to him, *"Thy sins be forgiven thee"* (Matt. 9:5), after which He added, *"Arise, take up thy bed, and go."* The pardon of sin and the healing of sickness complete one another, for in the eyes of God, who sees our entire natures, sin and sickness are as closely united as the body and the soul.

With us, sin belongs to the spiritual domain; we recognize that sin is under God's just displeasure, and that it is justly condemned by Him. Sickness, on the contrary, seems only a part of the present condition of our natures, having nothing to do with God's condemnation and His righteousness. Some go so far as to say that sickness is a proof of the love and grace of God.

But neither the Scripture nor Jesus Christ Himself ever speaks of sickness in this light, nor do they ever present sickness as a blessing, as proof of God's love that should be borne with patience. The Lord spoke to the disciples of various sufferings that they would have to bear, but when He spoke of sickness, it was always as an evil caused by sin and Satan, from which we should be delivered. Very solemnly, He declared that every disciple of His would have to bear his cross (Matt. 16:24), but He never taught one sick person to resign himself to being sick.

Everywhere, Jesus healed the sick; everywhere, He dealt with healing as one of the graces belonging to the kingdom of heaven. Sin in the soul and sickness in the body both bear witness to the power of Satan, and *"the Son of God was manifested that he might destroy the works of the devil"* (1 John 3:8).

Jesus came to deliver men from sin and sickness so that He might make known the love of the Father. In His actions, in His teaching of the disciples, and in the work of the apostles, pardon and healing were always found together. Their appearance depended on the development, or the faith, of those to whom they spoke. Sometimes healing prepared the way for the acceptance of forgiveness; sometimes forgiveness preceded healing, which, coming afterward, sealed it.

In the early part of His ministry, Jesus cured many of the sick, finding them eager to believe in the possibility of their healing. In this way, He sought to influence hearts to receive Him as One who could also pardon sin. When He saw that the paralytic could receive pardon at once, He pardoned him, because that was of the greatest importance. Then came the healing, which put a seal on the pardon he had been given.

Divine Healing

We see, in the accounts given in the Gospels, that it was more difficult for the Jews at that time to believe in the pardon of their sins than in divine healing. Now, it is just the opposite. The Christian church has heard so much preaching about the forgiveness of sins that the thirsty soul easily receives this message of grace. But it is not the same with divine healing, which is rarely mentioned. The believers who have experienced it are not many.

Healing is not always given in this day as it was in those times, to the multitudes whom Christ healed without any previous conversion. In order to receive healing, it is usually necessary to begin by confessing sin and desiring to live a holy life. This is without doubt the reason people find it more difficult to believe in healing than in forgiveness. This is also why those who receive healing receive at the same time new spiritual blessings; they feel more closely united to the Lord Jesus and learn to love and serve Him better. Unbelief may attempt to separate these two gifts, but they are always united in Christ. He is always the same Savior both of the soul and of the body, equally ready to grant pardon and healing. The redeemed may always cry, *"Bless the Lord, O my soul...who forgiveth all thine iniquities; who healeth all thy diseases"* (Ps. 103:2–3).

Two

Because of Your Unbelief

Then came the disciples to Jesus apart, and said,
Why could not we cast him out? And Jesus said unto them,
Because of your unbelief: for verily I say unto you,
If ye have faith as a grain of mustard seed,
ye shall say unto this mountain, Remove hence to yonder
place, and it shall remove,
and nothing shall be impossible to you.
—Matthew 17:19–20

When the Lord Jesus sent His disciples into different parts of Palestine, He endued them with a double power, to cast out unclean spirits and to heal all sickness and all infirmity (Matt. 10:1). He did the same for the seventy who came back to Him with joy, saying, *"Lord, even the devils are subject unto us through thy name"* (Luke 10:17). On the day of the Transfiguration, while the Lord was still on the mountain, a father brought his son who was possessed with a demon to His disciples, beseeching them to cast out the evil spirit, but they could not.

After Jesus had cured the child, the disciples asked why they had been unable to do it themselves, as they had in other cases. He answered them, *"Because of your unbelief."* It was their unbelief, and not the will of God, that had been the cause of their defeat.

In our day, divine healing is very little believed in because it has almost entirely disappeared from the Christian church. One may ask the reason, and here are the two answers that have been given. The greater number think that miracles—the gift of healing included—should be limited to the time of the early church, that their purpose was to establish the foundation of Christianity, but that from that time, circumstances have changed.

Other believers say unhesitatingly that if the church has lost these gifts, it is her own fault. It is because she has become worldly that the Spirit acts so feebly in her. It is because she has not remained in a direct and habitual relationship with the full power of the unseen world. But if men and women would spring up in her, living the life of faith and of the Holy Spirit, entirely consecrated to their God, she would see again the manifestation of the same gifts as in former times.

Which of these two opinions coincides with the Word of God? Is it by the will of God that the *"gifts of healing"* (1 Cor. 12:9) have been suppressed, or is it man who is responsible for the lack of healings? Is it the will of God that miracles should not take place? If this is so, will He no longer give the faith that produces them? Or again, is it the church that has been guilty of lacking faith?

The Bible does not authorize us, either by the words of the Lord or His apostles, to believe that the gifts of healing were granted only to the early church. On the contrary, the promise that Jesus made to the apostles shortly before His ascension, when He gave them instructions concerning their mission, appears to be applicable to all times. (See Mark 16:15–18.) Paul placed the gift of healing among the operations of the Holy Spirit. James gave a precise command on this matter without any restriction of time. The entire Scriptures declare that these graces will be granted according to the measure of the Spirit and of faith.

It is also alleged that at the outset of each new dispensation God works miracles, and that it is His ordinary course of action. But it is nothing of the kind. Think of the people of God in the former dispensation, in the time of Abraham, all through the life of Moses, in the Exodus from Egypt, under Joshua, in the time of the Judges and of Samuel, under the reign of David and other godly kings up to Daniel's time. During more than a thousand years, miracles took place.

It is said that miracles were much more necessary in the early days of Christianity than later. But what about the power of heathenism even in this day, wherever the Gospel seeks to combat it? It is impossible to conclude that miracles would have been more necessary for the heathen in Ephesus (Acts 19:11–12) than for the heathen scattered throughout the world today. Ignorance and unbelief reign even in the midst of Christian nations.

Are we not driven to say that there is a need for manifest acts of the power of God to sustain the testimony of believers and to prove that God is with them? Besides, among believers themselves, how much doubt and how much weakness there is! How their faith needs to be awakened and stimulated by some evidence of the presence of the Lord in their midst! One part of our being consists of flesh and blood; it is therefore in our flesh and blood that God wills to manifest His presence.

In order to prove that it is the church's unbelief that has lost the gift of healing, let us see what the Bible says about it. Does it not often put us on our guard against unbelief, against all that can estrange and turn us from our God? The history of the church shows us the necessity of these warnings. It furnishes us with numerous examples of backward steps—of world-pleasing—in which faith was weakened to the same extent that the spirit of the world took the upper hand. Faith is possible only to him who lives in the spiritual world.

Until the third century, healings by faith in Christ were numerous, but in the centuries following, they became more infrequent. Do we not know from the Bible that it is always unbelief that hinders the mighty working of God?

Oh, that we could learn to believe in the promise of God! God does not go back on His promises.

Jesus still heals both soul and body. Even now, salvation offers us healing and holiness, and the Holy Spirit is always ready to give us some manifestations of His power. When we ask why this divine power is not seen more often, He answers us, *"Because of your unbelief."* The more we allow ourselves to personally experience sanctification by faith, the more we also experience healing by faith. These two doctrines work together. The more the Spirit of God lives and acts in the souls of believers, the more miracles He will work in the body. By this, the world will recognize what redemption means.

Three

Jesus and the Doctors

*Now a certain woman had a flow of blood for twelve years,
and had suffered many things from many physicians. She
had spent all that she had and was no better, but rather
grew worse. When she heard about Jesus, she came behind
Him in the crowd and touched His garment. For she said,
"If only I may touch His clothes, I shall be made well."
Immediately the fountain of her blood was dried up, and
she felt in her body that she was healed of the affliction.
And Jesus, immediately knowing in Himself that power had
gone out of Him, turned around in the crowd and
said,..."Daughter, your faith has made you well. Go in
peace, and be healed of your affliction."*
—Mark 5:25–30, 34 NKJV

We may be thankful to God for giving us doctors.
Their vocation is one of the most noble, for a
large number of them truly seek to do—with love
and compassion—all they can do to alleviate the suffering that burdens humanity as a result of sin.
There are even some who are zealous servants of Jesus Christ, seeking also the good of their patients'

souls. Nevertheless, it is Jesus Himself who is always the first, the best, and the greatest Physician.

Jesus heals diseases in which earthly physicians can do nothing, for the Father gave Him this power when He charged Him with the work of our redemption. Jesus, in taking our human body upon Himself, delivered it from the dominion of sin and Satan. He has made our bodies temples of the Holy Spirit, and members of His own body (1 Cor. 6:15, 19). Even in our day, how many have been given up by the doctors as incurable? How many cases of cancer, infection, paralysis, heart disease, blindness, and deafness have been healed by Him? Is it not then astonishing that so small a number of the sick come to Him?

Jesus' method is quite different from that of earthly physicians. They seek to serve God in making use of remedies that are found in the natural world, according to the natural properties of each, while the healing that proceeds from Jesus is of a totally different order. It is by divine power—the power of the Holy Spirit—that Jesus heals. The difference between these two ways of healing is very striking.

In order to understand it better, consider this example: here is a physician who is an unbeliever, but extremely clever in his profession. Many sick people owe their healing to him. God gives this result by means of the prescribed remedies and the physician's knowledge of them. Here is another physician who is a believer, and who prays God's blessing on the remedies that he employs. In this case also, a large number are healed, but in neither case does the healing bring with it any spiritual blessing. They will be preoccupied, even the believing among them, with the remedies that they use much more than with what the Lord may be doing with them. In some instances, their healing may be more hurtful than beneficial to their spiritual lives. On the other hand, when it is Jesus alone to whom the sick person applies for healing, he learns to rely no longer on remedies, but to put himself into direct contact with His love and His almightiness. In order to obtain such healing, he must begin by confessing and renouncing his sins, and exercising a living faith. Then, healing will come directly from the Lord, who takes possession of the sick body. It thus becomes a blessing for the soul as well as for the body.

"But is it not God who has given medical treatments to man?" it is asked. "Doesn't their power come from Him?" Without a doubt it does. But on the other hand, is it not God who has given us His Son with all power to heal? Will we follow the way of natural law with all those who do not yet know Christ, and also with those of His children whose faith is still too weak to abandon themselves to His almightiness? Or, rather, do we choose the way of faith, receiving healing from the Lord and from the Holy Spirit, seeing therein the result and the proof of our redemption?

The healing that is brought about by our Lord Jesus brings with it and leaves behind it more real blessing than the healing that is obtained through physicians. Healing that relied on human means alone has been a misfortune to the spiritual lives of more persons than one. Although thoughts of the Lord may cross the sick man's mind while he's still on his sickbed, once he has been healed, he finds himself far from the Lord.

Divine Healing

It is not that way when it is Jesus who heals.

Healing is granted after confession of sin; therefore, it brings the sufferer nearer to Jesus, and it establishes a new link between him and the Lord. It causes him to experience His love and power; it begins within him a new life of faith and holiness. When the woman who had touched the hem of Christ's garment felt that she was healed, she learned something of what divine love means. She went away, possessing the words, *"Daughter, thy faith hath made thee whole; go in peace."*

O you who are suffering from some sickness, know that Jesus, the sovereign Healer, is yet in our midst. He is close to us, and He is giving many new proofs of His presence to His church. Are you ready to break with the world, to abandon yourself to Him with faith and confidence? Then fear not.

Remember that divine healing is a part of the life of faith. If nobody around you can help you in prayer, if no "elder" is at hand to pray the prayer of faith, do not be afraid to go to the Lord yourself in the silence of solitude, like the woman who touched the hem of His garment. Commit the care of your body to Him. Get quiet before Him, and like the poor woman, say, "I will be healed." Perhaps it may take some time to break the chains of your unbelief, but assuredly none who wait on Him will be ashamed (Ps. 25:3).

Four

Health and Salvation
by the Name of Jesus

*And His name, through faith in His name, has made this
man strong, whom you see and know. Yes, the faith which
comes through Him has given him this perfect soundness in
the presence of you all.*
—Acts 3:16 NKJV

*Be it known unto you all, and to all the people of Israel,
that by the name of Jesus Christ of Nazareth, whom ye
crucified, whom God raised from the dead, even by him
doth this man stand here before you whole....Neither
is there salvation in any other: for there is none
other name under heaven given among men,
whereby we must be saved.*
—Acts 4:10, 12

After Pentecost, the paralytic was healed through
Peter and John at the gate of the temple. It was
"in the name of Jesus Christ of Nazareth" that they
said to him, *"Rise up and walk"* (Acts 3:6). As soon
as the people in their amazement ran together to

them, Peter declared that it was the name of Jesus that had so completely healed the man.

As a result of this miracle and of Peter's discourse, many people who had heard the Word believed (Acts 4:4). The next day, Peter repeated these words before the Sanhedrin: *"By the name of Jesus Christ of Nazareth...doth this man stand here before you whole"*; and then he added, *"There is none other name under heaven...whereby we must be saved."* This statement of Peter declares to us that the name of Jesus both heals and saves. We have here a teaching of the highest importance for divine healing.

We see that healing and health form part of Christ's salvation. Peter clearly stated this in his discourse to the Sanhedrin where, having spoken of healing, he immediately went on to speak of salvation by Christ. (See Acts 4:10, 12.) In heaven, even our bodies will have their part in salvation. Salvation will not be complete for us until our bodies enjoy the full redemption of Christ. Shouldn't we believe in this work of redemption here below? Even here on earth, the health of our bodies is a fruit of the salvation that Jesus has acquired for us.

We also see that health, as well as salvation, is to be obtained by faith. The tendency of man by nature is to bring about his own salvation by his works, and it is only with difficulty that he comes to receive it by faith. But when it is a question of the healing of the body, he has still more difficulty in seizing it. He finally accepts salvation, because by no other means can he open the door of heaven. But it is much easier for him to accept well-known remedies for his body. Why, then, should he seek divine healing?

Health and Salvation

Happy is he who comes to understand that it is the will of God to heal, to manifest the power of Jesus, and to reveal to us His fatherly love. It is also His will that we exercise and confirm our faith, to make us prove the power of redemption in the body as well as in the soul. The body is part of our being. Even the body has been saved by Christ. Therefore, it is in our bodies that our Father wills to manifest the power of redemption, and to let men see that Jesus lives. Oh, let us believe in the name of Jesus! Was it not in the name of Jesus that perfect health was given to the crippled man? And were not the words *"Your faith has made you well"* (Mark 5:34 NKJV) pronounced when the woman with the issue of blood was healed? Let us seek, then, to obtain divine healing.

Wherever the Spirit acts with power, He works divine healings. If ever there was an abundance of miracles, it was at Pentecost, for then the word of the apostles worked mightily, and the pouring out of the Holy Spirit was great. Well, it is precisely because the Spirit acted powerfully that His working was so visible in the body. If divine healing is seen but rarely in our day, we can attribute it to no other cause than that the Spirit does not act with power. The unbelief of worldlings and the lack of zeal among believers stop His working. The healings that God is giving here and there are the initial signs of all the spiritual graces that are promised to us, and it is only the Holy Spirit who reveals the almightiness of the name of Jesus to operate such healings. Let us pray earnestly for the Holy Spirit, let us place ourselves unreservedly under His direction, and let us seek to be firm in our faith in the name of Jesus, whether for preaching salvation or for the work of healing.

God grants healing to glorify the name of Jesus. Let us seek to be healed by Jesus, so that His name may be glorified. It is sad to see how little the power of His name is recognized, how little it is used in preaching and prayer. Treasures of divine grace—of which Christians deprive themselves by their lack of faith and zeal—are hidden in the name of Jesus.

It is the will of God to glorify His Son in the church, and He will do it wherever He finds faith. Whether among believers or among the heathen, He is ready with virtue from on high to awaken consciences and to bring hearts to obedience. God is ready to manifest the power of His Son, and to do it in striking ways in bodies as well as in souls. Let us believe it for ourselves; let us believe it for others, for the circle of believers around us, and also for the church in the whole world. Let us give ourselves to believe with firm faith in the power of the name of Jesus. Let us ask great things in His name, counting on His promise, and we will see that God still does wonders by the name of His holy Son.

Five

Not by Our Own Power

And when Peter saw it, he answered unto the people, Ye
men of Israel why marvel ye at this? or why look ye so
earnestly on us, as though by our own power or holiness we
had made this man to walk?
—Acts 3:12

As soon as the crippled man had been healed at
the gate of the temple, the people ran together to
Peter and John. Peter, seeing this miracle was at-
tributed to their power and holiness, lost no time in
setting them right by telling them that all the glory
of this miracle belonged to Jesus, and that it is He in
whom we must believe.

Peter and John were undoubtedly full of faith
and of holiness; they may have been the holiest and
most zealous servants of God in their time. Otherwise, God might not have chosen them as instru-
ments in this case of healing. But they knew that
their holiness of life was not of themselves, that it was
of God through the Holy Spirit. They thought so little
of themselves that they ignored their own holiness

and knew only one thing—that all power belonged to their Master. They hastened, then, to declare that in this act of healing, their efforts counted for nothing; it was the work of the Lord alone! This is the purpose of divine healing: to be a proof of the power of Jesus, to be a witness in the eyes of men of what He is, proclaiming His divine intervention and attracting hearts to Him. Those whom the Lord uses in helping others should remember Peter's words: "[Not] *by our own power or holiness.*"

It is necessary to insist on this because of the tendency of believers to think the contrary. Those who have recovered their health in answer to *"the prayer of faith"* (James 5:15) and *"the effectual fervent prayer of a righteous man"* (v. 16) are in danger of being too much occupied with the human instrument that God is pleased to employ, and to think that the power lies in man's piety.

Doubtless the prayer of faith is the result of real godliness, but those who possess it will be the first to acknowledge that it does not come from themselves, nor from any efforts of their own. They fear to rob the Lord of the least particle of the glory that belongs to Him. They know that if they do so, they will compel Him to withdraw His grace from them. It is their great desire to see the souls that God has blessed through them enter into a direct and increasingly intimate communion with the Lord Jesus Christ Himself, since that is the result that their healing should produce. Thus they insist that it is not caused by their own power or holiness.

Such testimony on their part is necessary to reply to the erroneous accusations of unbelievers. The

church of Christ needs to hear clearly announced
that it is because of her worldliness and unbelief that
she has lost these spiritual gifts of healing (1 Cor.
12:9), and that the Lord restores those gifts to those
who, with faith and obedience, have consecrated
their lives to Him. This grace cannot reappear, however, without being preceded by a renewal of faith
and of holiness. But then, says the world, and with it
a large number of Christians, "You are laying claim
to the possession of a higher order of faith and holiness; you consider yourselves holier than others." To
such accusations, this word of Peter is the only reply
before God and before man, confirmed by a life of
deep and real humility: "[Not] *by our own power or
holiness.*" "*Not unto us, O Lord, not unto us, but
unto thy name give glory, for thy mercy, and for thy
truth's sake*" (Ps. 115:1).

Such a testimony is necessary also in view of our
own hearts and the wiles of Satan. As long as,
through the church's unfaithfulness, the gifts of
healing are but rarely given, those children of God
who do receive these gifts are in danger of taking
pride in them, imagining that they are somehow special. The Enemy does not forget to persecute them
by such insinuations, and woe unto them if they listen to him. They should be made aware of his de-
vices. Then, they need to pray continually to the
Lord to keep them in humility, the true means of obtaining continually more grace. If they persevere in
humility, they will recognize that the more God
makes use of them, the more they will be penetrated
with the conviction that it is God alone who works
by them, and that all the glory belongs to Him. "*Not*

I, but the grace of God which was with me" (1 Cor. 15:10)—such is their watchword.

Finally, this testimony is useful for the weaker ones who long for salvation and who desire to receive Christ as their Healer. They hear of full consecration and entire obedience, but they form a false idea of it. They think they must attain such a high degree of knowledge and of perfection that they become discouraged. Remember this: it is not by our own power or holiness that we obtain grace, but by a faith quite simple—a childlike faith—that knows that it has no power or holiness of its own, and that commits itself completely to Him. He is faithful, and His almightiness can fulfill His promise. Oh, let us not seek to do or to be anything of ourselves! It is only as we feel our own powerlessness, and expect everything from God and His Word, that we realize the glorious way in which the Lord heals sickness by faith in His name.

According to the Measure of Faith

And Jesus said unto the centurion, Go thy way, and as
thou hast believed, so be it done unto thee. And his
servant was healed in the same hour.
—Matthew 8:13

This passage of Scripture brings us one of the principal laws of the kingdom of heaven. In order to understand God's ways with His people and our relationship with the Lord, it is necessary to understand this law thoroughly and not to deviate from it. Not only does God give or withhold His grace according to the faith or unbelief of each, but also it is granted in greater or lesser measure in proportion to the faith that receives it. Therefore, He can bless us only to the extent to which each believer yields himself up to His divine working and opens all his heart to Him. Faith in God is nothing less than the full opening of the heart to receive everything from God. Therefore, man can receive divine grace only according to his faith. This applies as much to divine healing as to any other grace of God.

Divine Healing

This truth is confirmed by the spiritual blessings that may result from sickness. Two questions are often asked. First, is it not God's will that His children should sometimes remain in a prolonged state of sickness? Second, since it is recognized that divine healing brings with it greater spiritual blessing than the sickness itself, why does God allow some of His children to remain sick for many years, and while in this condition, still bless them in communion with Himself? The answer to these two questions is that God gives to His children according to their faith.

We have already had occasion to remark that in the same degree to which the church has become worldly, her faith in divine healing has diminished, until at last it has almost disappeared. Believers do not seem to be aware that they may ask God for the healing of their sickness, and that, through their healing, they may be sanctified and equipped for His service. They have come to seek only submission to His will and to regard sickness as a means to be separate from the world. In such conditions, the Lord gives them what they ask. He would have been willing to give them much more—to grant them healing in answer to the prayer of faith—but they lacked the faith to receive it.

God always meets His children where they are, however weak they may be. The sick ones, therefore, who have desired to be submissive to His will at all costs will enjoy a deep inner communion with Him.

But they might have been able to receive healing, in addition, as a proof that God accepted their submission. If this has not happened, it is because faith has failed them to ask for it.

According to the Measure of Faith

"As thou hast believed, so be it done unto thee." These words give the reply to yet another question: How can you say that divine healing brings so much spiritual blessing with it, when one sees that the greater number of those who were healed by the Lord Jesus received nothing more than a deliverance from their present sufferings, without giving any proof that they were also spiritually blessed? Here again, as they believed, so was it done unto them.

A good number of sick people, having witnessed the healing of others, gained just enough confidence in Jesus to be healed. Jesus granted them their request, without adding other blessings for their souls. Before His ascension, the Lord did not have as free an entrance as He now has into the heart of man, because *"the Holy Ghost was not yet given"* (John 7:39). The healing of the sick was then hardly more than a blessing for the body. It was only later, with the dispensation of the Spirit, that the conviction and confession of sin have become, for the believer, the first grace to be received, the essential condition for obtaining healing. Paul told us this in his epistle to the Corinthians, and James in his to the twelve tribes scattered abroad. (See 1 Corinthians 11:31–32; James 5:16.) Thus, the degree of spiritual grace that it is possible for us to receive depends on the amount of our faith, whether it be for its external manifestation or for its influence on our inner lives.

We commend, then, to every suffering one who is looking for healing and seeking to know Jesus as his divine Healer, not to let himself be hindered by his unbelief and not to doubt the promises of God. Be strong in faith, giving glory to God as is His due. *"As thou hast believed, so be it done unto thee."* If with all your heart you trust in the living God, you will be abundantly blessed. Do not doubt it.

Faith's part is to grasp that which appears impossible or strange to human eyes. Let us be willing to be considered fools for Christ's sake (1 Cor. 4:10). Let us not fear to be considered weak-minded in the eyes of the world and of uninformed Christians because, on the authority of the Word of God, we believe what others cannot yet admit. Do not, then, let yourself be discouraged in your expectation, even though God should delay to answer you, or your sickness should seem to worsen.

Place your feet firmly on the immovable rock of God's own Word. Pray to the Lord to manifest His almightiness in your body because you are one of the members of His body (see 1 Corinthians 12) and *"the temple of the Holy Spirit"* (1 Cor. 6:19). Persevere in believing in Him with the firm assurance that He has undertaken for you, that He has made Himself responsible for your body, and that His healing power will glorify Him in you even as it heals you.

Seven

The Way of Faith

*And straightway the father of the child cried out, and said
with tears, Lord, I believe; help thou mine unbelief.*
—Mark 9:24

These words have been a help and strength to
thousands of souls in their pursuit of salvation
and the gifts of God. Notice that it is in relation to
an afflicted child that they were said, as the child's
father fought the fight of faith and sought healing
from the Lord Jesus. In them, we see that in one and
the same soul a struggle between faith and unbelief
can occur. It is not without a struggle that we come
to believe in Jesus and in His complete power to heal
the sick. In this truth, we find the necessary encour-
agement for realizing the Savior's power.

I speak here especially to sufferers who do not
doubt the power or the will of the Lord Jesus to heal
in this day, but who lack the boldness to accept
healing for themselves. They believe in the divine
power of Christ; they believe in His goodwill to heal;
they believe, either from the Scriptures or from pre-
sent-day healings, that the Lord can help even them,

but they shrink back from accepting healing. They cannot say with faith, "The Lord has heard me. I know that He is healing me."

Take notice, first, that without faith no one can be healed. When the father of the afflicted child said to Jesus, *"If thou canst do any thing, have compassion on us, and help us"* (Mark 9:22), Jesus replied, *"If thou canst believe"* (v. 23). Jesus had the power to heal, and He was ready to do it, but He cast responsibility on the man. *"If you can believe, all things are possible to him who believes"* (v. 23 NKJV).

In order to obtain your healing from Jesus, it is not enough to pray. Prayer without faith is powerless. It is *"the prayer of faith"* that saves the sick (James 5:15). If you have already asked for healing from the Lord, or if others have asked it for you, you must, before you are conscious of any change, be able to say with faith, "On the authority of God's Word, I have the assurance that He hears me and that I am healed." To have faith means to surrender your body absolutely into the Lord's hands, and to leave yourself entirely to Him. Faith receives healing as a spiritual grace that proceeds from the Lord, even while there is no conscious change in the body. Faith can glorify God and say, *"Bless the Lord, O my soul... who healeth all my diseases"* (Ps. 103:1, 3). The Lord requires this faith so that He may heal.

But how is such faith to be obtained? Tell God of the unbelief that you find in your heart, and count on Him for deliverance from it. Faith is not money by which your healing can be purchased from the Lord. It is He who desires to awaken and develop in you the necessary faith. "Help my unbelief," cried the father of the child. It was his ardent desire that his faith should not come short.

Confess to the Lord all the difficulty you have in believing Him on the ground of His Word. Tell Him you want to be rid of this unbelief, that you bring it to Him with a will to listen only to His Word. Do not lose time in deploring your unbelief, but look to Jesus. The light of His countenance will enable you to find the power to believe in Him (Ps. 43:3). He calls on you to trust in Him. Listen to Him and, by His grace, faith will triumph in you. Say to Him, "Lord, I am still aware of the unbelief that is in me. I find it difficult to believe that I am assured of my healing just because I possess Him who works it in me. Nevertheless, I want to conquer this unbelief. You, Lord, will give me the victory. I desire to believe, I will believe, and by Your grace, I can believe. Yes, Lord, I believe, for You help me with my unbelief." It is when we are in intimate communion with the Lord, and when our hearts respond to His, that unbelief is overcome and conquered.

It is necessary to testify to the faith one has. Believe what the Lord says to you and believe, above all, what He is. Lean completely on His promises.

"The prayer of faith shall save the sick" (James 5:15). *"I am the LORD that healeth thee"* (Exod. 15:26). Look to Jesus, who *"bare our sicknesses"* (Matt. 8:17) and who healed all who came to Him. Count on the Holy Spirit to manifest the presence of Jesus in your heart, and to work the power of His grace in your body. Praise the Lord without waiting to feel better or to have more faith. Praise Him, and say with David, *"O Lord, my God, I cried unto thee, and thou hast healed me"* (Ps. 30:2).

Divine Healing

Divine healing is a spiritual grace that can only be received spiritually and by faith, before its effect is felt on the body. Accept it, then, and give glory to God. When the Lord Jesus had commanded the unclean spirit to come out of the child, many of the onlookers believed the child had died. If, therefore, your sickness does not yield at once, or if Satan and your own unbelief attempt to get the upper hand, do not heed them. Cling closely to Jesus your Healer, and He will surely heal you.

Eight

Your Body Is the Temple
of the Holy Spirit

Do you not know that your bodies are members of Christ?
Shall I then take the members of Christ and make them
members of a harlot? Certainly not!...Or do you not know
that your body is the temple of the Holy Spirit who is in you,
whom you have from God, and you are not your own? For
you were bought at a price; therefore glorify God in your
body and in your spirit, which are God's.
—1 Corinthians 6:15, 19–20 NKJV

The Bible teaches us that the body of Christ is the company of the faithful. These words are generally taken in their spiritual sense, but the Bible asks us specifically whether we know that our bodies are the members of Christ. In the same way, when the Bible speaks of the indwelling of the Holy Spirit or of Christ, we limit His presence to the spiritual part of our being. Nevertheless, the Bible says expressly, *"Do you not know that your body is the temple of the Holy Spirit?"* The church needs to understand that the body also has part in the redemption that is by Christ, by which it ought to be brought back to its original destiny, to be the dwelling place of the Holy Spirit, to serve as His instrument, and to be sanctified by His presence. The church must also recognize the place that divine healing has in the Bible and in the counsels of God.

The account of creation tells us that man is composed of three parts. God first formed the body from the dust of the earth, after which He breathed into it *"the breath of life"* (Gen. 2:7). He caused His own life, His Spirit, to enter into it. By this union of Spirit with matter, the man became *"a living soul"* (v. 7). The soul, which is essentially the man, finds its place between the body and the spirit; it is the link that binds them together. By the body, the soul finds itself in relation to the external world; by the spirit, it relates with the invisible world and with God. By means of the soul, the spirit can subject the body to the action of the heavenly powers and, thus, spiritualize it; by means of the soul, the body also can act on the spirit and attract it earthward. The soul, subject to the solicitations of both spirit and body, is in a position to choose between the voice of God, speaking to the spirit, or the voice of the world, speaking through the senses.

This union of spirit and body forms a combination that is unique in the creation. It makes man the jewel of God's work. Other creatures had existed already. Some were like angels—all spirit, without any material body. Others, like the animals, were only flesh, possessing a body animated with a living soul, but devoid of spirit. Man was destined to show that the material body, governed by the spirit, was capable of being transformed by the power of the Spirit of

God, and of being thus led to participate in heavenly glory.

We know what sin and Satan have done with this possibility of gradual transformation. By means of the body, the spirit was tempted and seduced; it became a slave of the senses. We know also what God has done to destroy the work of Satan and to accomplish the purpose of creation. *"The Son of God was manifested, that he might destroy the works of the devil"* (1 John 3:8). God prepared a body for His Son (Heb. 10:5). *"The Word was made flesh"* (John 1:14). *"In him dwelleth all the fulness of the Godhead bodily"* (Col. 2:9). *"Who his own self bare our sins in his own body on the tree"* (1 Pet. 2:24). And now Jesus, raised up from the dead with a body as free from sin as His spirit and His soul, communicates to our bodies the virtue of His glorified body. The Lord's Supper is *"the communion of the body of Christ"* (1 Cor. 10:16), and our bodies are *"the members of Christ"* (1 Cor. 6:15).

Faith puts us in possession of everything that the death of Christ and His resurrection obtained for us. It is not only in our spirits and our souls that the life of the risen Jesus manifests its presence here below, but also in our bodies, according to our faith.

"Do you not know that your body is the temple of the Holy Spirit?" Many believers imagine that the Holy Spirit comes to dwell in our bodies as one dwells in a house. This comparison is not a good one. I can dwell in a house without its becoming part of my being. I may leave it without suffering; no vital union exists between my house and me. It is not this way with the presence of our souls and spirits in our bodies.

Divine Healing

The life of a plant lives and animates every part of it. In the same way, our souls are not limited to dwell in such or such a part of the body—the heart or the head, for instance. It penetrates throughout, even to the ends of the lowest members. The life of the soul pervades the whole body; the life throughout proves the presence of the soul. It is in like manner that the Holy Spirit comes to dwell in our bodies. He penetrates them entirely. He animates and possesses us infinitely more than we can imagine.

In the same way that the Holy Spirit brings to our souls and spirits the life of Jesus—His holiness, His joy, His strength—He comes also to impart to the sick body all the vigorous vitality of Christ as soon as the hand of faith is stretched out to receive it. When the body is fully subjected to Christ, crucified with Him, renouncing all self-will and independence, desiring nothing but to be the Lord's temple, it is then that the Holy Spirit manifests the power of the risen Savior in the body. Only then can we glorify God in our bodies, leaving Him full freedom to manifest His power in us, to show that He knows how to set His temple free from the domination of sickness, sin, and Satan.

Nine

The Body for the Lord

*Meats for the belly, and the belly for meats: but God shall
destroy both it and them. Now the body is not for
fornication, but for the Lord, and the Lord for the body.*
—1 Corinthians 6:13

O ne of the most knowledgeable theologians has
said that the redemption and glorification of
the body is the end of the ways of God. As we have
already seen, this is indeed what God has accomplished in creating man. It is this that makes the in-
habitants of heaven wonder and admire when they
contemplate the glory of the Son. Clothed with a glorified human body, Jesus has taken His place forever
on the throne of God, to share His glory. It is this
that God has willed. It shall be recognized in that
day when regenerated humanity, forming the body
of Christ, shall be truly and visibly the temple of the
living God (1 Cor. 6:19). All creation in the new
heavens and the new earth will share the glory of the
children of God. The material body will then be
wholly sanctified and glorified by the Spirit. This

body, thus spiritualized, will be the highest glory of the Lord Jesus Christ and of His redeemed.

It is in anticipation of this new condition of things that the Lord attaches a great importance to the indwelling and sanctification of our bodies, here on earth, by His Spirit. This truth is so little understood by believers that they seek the power of the Holy Spirit in their bodies even less. Many of them, believing that this body belongs to them, use it as it pleases them. Not understanding how much the sanctification of the soul and spirit depends on the body, they do not grasp the meaning of the words, "The body is for the Lord," in such a way as to receive them in obedience.

"The body is for the Lord." What does this mean? The apostle had just said, *"Meats for the belly, and the belly for meats: but God shall destroy both it and them."* Eating and drinking afford the Christian an opportunity of carrying out this truth, "The body is for the Lord." He must indeed learn to eat and drink to the glory of God. By eating, sin and the Fall came about. It was also through eating that the Devil sought to tempt our Lord. Thus Jesus Himself sanctified His body in eating only according to the will of His Father (Matt. 4:4). Many believers fail to watch over their bodies, to observe a holy sobriety through the fear of rendering it unfit for the service of God. Eating and drinking should never impede communion with God. On the contrary, they should help us maintain the body in its normal condition. The apostle spoke also of fornication, this sin that defiles the body, and that is in direct opposition to the words, "The body is for the Lord." It is not simply sexual promiscuity outside the married state, but all voluptuousness, all lack of sobriety regarding sensual pleasure is condemned in these words: *"Your body is the temple of the Holy Ghost"* (1 Cor. 6:19). In the same way, all that goes to maintain the body—to clothe it, strengthen it, give it rest or enjoyment—should be placed under the control of the Holy Spirit. Just as, under the old covenant, the temple was constructed solely for God and for His service, even so our bodies have been created for the Lord and for Him alone.

One of the chief benefits, then, of divine healing is to teach us that our bodies ought to be set free from the yoke of our own wills to become the Lord's property. God does not grant healing to our prayers until He has attained the end for which He had permitted the sickness. He wills that this discipline bring us into a more intimate communion with Him. He wants us to understand that we have regarded our bodies as our own property, while they actually belong to the Lord, and that the Holy Spirit seeks to sanctify all their actions. He leads us to understand that if we yield our bodies unreservedly to the influence of the Holy Spirit, we will experience His power in us, and He will heal us by bringing into our bodies the very life of Jesus. He leads us, in short, to say with full conviction, "The body is for the Lord."

There are believers who seek holiness, but only for the soul and spirit. In their ignorance, they forget that the body and all its systems—and even the hands, the ears, the eyes, and the mouth—are called to testify directly to the presence and the grace of God in them. They have not sufficiently taken in these words: *"Your bodies are the members of Christ"* (v. 15). *"If ye through the Spirit do mortify the deeds of the body, ye shall live"* (Rom. 8:13). *"And the very God of peace sanctify you wholly; and I pray God your whole spirit and soul and body be preserved blameless unto the coming of our Lord Jesus Christ"* (1 Thess. 5:23).

Oh, what a renewing takes place in us when, by His own touch, the Lord heals our bodies, when He takes possession of them, and when, by His Spirit, He becomes life and health to them! It is with an indescribable consciousness of holiness, of fear, and of joy that the believer can then offer his body a living sacrifice to receive healing, and to have for his motto these words: "The body is for the Lord."

Ten

The Lord for the Body

Meats for the belly, and the belly for meats: but God shall
destroy both it and them. Now the body is not for
fornication, but for the Lord, and the Lord for the body.
—1 Corinthians 6:13

There is reciprocity in God's relationship with man. What God has been for me, I ought, in my turn, to be for Him. And what I am for Him, He desires to be for me. If, in His love, He gives Himself fully to me, it is in order that I may lovingly give myself fully to Him. In the measure in which I really surrender myself to Him, in that measure, also, He gives Himself back to me. God thus leads the believer to understand that this abandonment of Himself is for our bodies.

The more our lives bear witness that our bodies are for the Lord, the more we experience that the Lord is for the body. In saying, "The body is for the Lord," we express the desire to regard our bodies as wholly consecrated, offered in sacrifice to the Lord, and sanctified by Him. In saying, "The Lord is for the body," we express the precious certainty that our

47

offering has been accepted. We show we believe that, by His Spirit, the Lord will impart to our bodies His own strength and holiness, and that henceforth He will strengthen and keep us.

This is a matter of faith. Our bodies are material, weak, feeble, sinful, and mortal. Therefore, it is difficult to grasp the full meaning of the words, "The Lord is for the body." It is the Word of God that enables us to do so. The body was created by the Lord and for the Lord. Jesus took upon Him an earthly body. In His body, He bore our sins on the cross, and thereby set our bodies free from the power of sin. In Christ, the body has been raised again and seated on the throne of God. The body is the habitation of the Holy Spirit; it is called to eternal partnership in the glory of heaven. Therefore, with certainty, and in a wide and universal sense, we can say, "Yes, the Lord Jesus, our Savior, is for the body."

This truth has various applications. In the first place, it is a great help in practical holiness. More than one sin derives its strength from some physical tendency. The recovering alcoholic has a horror of intoxicating drinks, but his appetites can still be a snare to him, gaining victory over his new convictions. If, however, in the conflict, he gives his body with confidence to the Lord, all physical appetite, all desire to drink will be overcome.

Our temper also often results from our physical constitution. A nervous, irritable system produces words that are sharp, harsh, and unloving. But let the body, with this physical tendency, be taken to the Lord, and the Holy Spirit will overcome the risings of impatience, and sanctify the body, rendering it blameless.

The Lord for the Body

These words, "The Lord is for the body," are applicable also to the physical strength that the Lord's service demands of us. When David cried, *"It is God that girdeth me with strength,"* he meant physical strength, for he added, *"He maketh my feet like hinds' feet....A bow of steel is broken by mine arms"* (Ps. 18:32–34). Again, these words, *"The LORD is the strength of my life"* (Ps. 27:1), do not refer only to the spiritual man, but to the entire man. Many believers have experienced that the promise, *"They that wait upon the LORD shall renew their strength"* (Isa. 40:31), touched their bodies, and that the Holy Spirit increased their physical strength.

But it is especially in divine healing that we see the truth of these words, "The Lord is for the body." Yes, Jesus, the sovereign and merciful Healer, is always ready to save and cure. In Switzerland some years ago, there was a young girl near death from tuberculosis. The doctor had advised a milder climate, but she was too weak to take the journey. She learned that Jesus is the Healer of the sick and believed the good news. One night when she was thinking of this subject, it seemed to her that the body of the Lord drew near to her, and that she ought to take these words literally, "His body for our body." From this moment, she began to improve. Some time after, she began to hold Bible readings, and later on she became a zealous and much blessed worker for the Lord among women. She had learned to understand that the Lord is for the body.

Dear sick one, the Lord has shown you by sickness what power sin has over the body. By your healing, He would like to show you the power of redemption of the body. He calls to show you what you have not understood until now, that "the body is for the Lord." Therefore, give Him your body. Give it to Him with your sickness and your sin, which is the original source of sickness. Always believe that the Lord has taken charge of this body, and He will manifest with power that He really is the Lord, who is for the body. The Lord, who took an earthly body and regenerated it, sends us His divine strength from the highest heaven, where He is now clothed in His glorified body. He is willing thus to manifest His power in our bodies.

Eleven

Do Not Consider Your Body

I speak after the manner of men because of the infirmity
of your flesh: for as ye have yielded your members
servants to uncleanness and to iniquity unto iniquity,
even so now yield your members servants to righteousness
unto holiness. For when ye were the servants of sin,
ye were free from righteousness. What fruit had ye then
in those things whereof ye are now ashamed?
for the end of those things is death.
—Romans 6:19–21

When God promised to give Abraham a son, the patriarch would never have been able to believe in this promise if he had considered his own body, already aged and worn out. But Abraham would see nothing but God and His promise. He looked to the power and faithfulness of God who guaranteed him the fulfillment of His promise.

This kind of faith enables us to lay hold of all the difference there is between the healing that is expected from earthly remedies alone and the healing that is looked for from God. When we use earthly remedies alone for healing, all the attention of the sick one is on the body. Divine healing, however, calls us to turn our attention away from the body, abandoning ourselves—soul and body—to the Lord's care, occupying ourselves with Him alone.

This truth also enables us to see the difference between the sickness retained for blessing and the healing received from the Lord. Some are afraid to take the promise in James, chapter five, in its literal sense because they say sickness is more profitable to the soul than health. It is true that in the case of healing obtained by earthly remedies, many people would be more spiritually blessed in remaining ill than in recovering health, but it is quite otherwise when healing comes directly from the hand of God. In order for the child of God to receive divine healing, the following usually must take place: sin must be confessed and renounced, one must completely surrender to the Lord, self must be yielded up to be wholly in His hands, and one must firmly believe that Jesus desires to take charge of the body. Then, the healing becomes the beginning of a new life of intimate communion with the Lord.

Thus we learn to relinquish the ultimate care of our health entirely to Him. The smallest indication of the return of the sickness is regarded as a warning not to consider our bodies, but to be occupied with the Lord only.

What a contrast this is from the greater number of sick people who look for healing from earthly remedies alone. Some of them may have been sanctified by the sickness, having learned to lose sight of themselves. But how many more are there who are drawn by the sickness itself to be constantly occupied with themselves and with the condition of their bodies? What infinite care they exercise in observing the least symptom, favorable or unfavorable. What a constant preoccupation to them is their eating and drinking—the anxiety to avoid this or that. How much they are taken up with what they consider is due to them from others—whether they are sufficiently thought of, whether well enough nursed, whether visited often enough. How much time is thus devoted to considering the body and what it needs, rather than to the Lord and the relationship that He seeks to establish with their souls. Oh, how many are they who, through sickness, are occupied almost exclusively with themselves!

All this is totally different when healing is sought for in faith from the loving God. Then the first thing to learn is to cease to be anxious about the state of your body. You have trusted it to the Lord, and He has taken the responsibility. If you do not see a rapid improvement immediately, but on the contrary the symptoms appear to be more serious, remember that you have entered on a path of faith, and therefore you should not consider the body, but cling only to the living God. The commandment of Christ, *"Do not worry about your...body"* (Matt. 6:25 NKJV), appears here in a new light. When God told Abraham not to consider his own body, it was so that He could call him to the greatest exercise of faith there is—to see only God and His promise. Sustained by his faith, he gave glory to God, convinced that God would do what He had promised.

Divine healing is a marvelous tie to bind us to the Lord. At first, one may fear to believe that the Lord will stretch forth His mighty hand and touch the body. But, in studying the Word of God, the soul takes courage and confidence. At last, one decides, saying, "I yield up my body into the hands of God, and I leave the care of it to Him." Then the body and its sensations are forgotten, and only the Lord and His promise are in view.

Dear reader, will you also enter this way of faith, very superior to that which is natural? Walk in the steps of Abraham. Learn from him not to consider your own body, and not to doubt through unbelief. To consider the body gives birth to doubts, while clinging to the promise of God and being occupied with Him alone gives entrance into the way of faith, the way of divine healing, which glorifies God.

Twelve

Discipline and Sanctification

God...chasteneth...us...for our profit, that we may be partakers of his holiness.
—Hebrews 12:7, 10

If a man...purge himself...he shall be a vessel unto honour, sanctified, and meet for the master's use, and prepared unto every good work.
—2 Timothy 2:21

To sanctify anything is to set it apart—to conse-crate it—to God and to His service. The temple at Jerusalem was holy; that is to say, it was conse-crated, dedicated to God to serve Him as a dwelling place. The vessels of the temple were holy, because they were devoted to the service of the temple. The priests were holy, chosen to serve God and ready to work for Him. In the same way, the Christian ought also to be sanctified, at the Lord's disposal, ready to do every good work.

When the people of Israel went out of Egypt, the Lord reclaimed them for His service as a holy people. *"Let my people go, that they may serve me"* (Exod.

7:16), He said to Pharaoh. Set free from their hard bondage, the children of Israel were debtors who immediately entered the service of God, becoming His happy servants. Their deliverance was the road that led to their sanctification.

Again in this day, God is forming a holy people for Himself, and Jesus sets us free so that we may join them. He *"gave Himself for us, that He might redeem us from every lawless deed and purify for Himself His own special people, zealous for good works"* (Titus 2:14 NKJV). It is the Lord who breaks the chains by which Satan tries to hold us in bondage. He wants us to be free, wholly free to serve Him. He wills to save us, to deliver both the soul and the body, so that each of the members of the body may be consecrated to Him and placed unreservedly at His disposal.

A large number of Christians do not yet understand all this. They cannot comprehend that the purpose of their deliverance is that they may be sanctified, prepared to serve their God. They make use of their lives and their bodies to obtain their own satisfaction; consequently, they do not feel at liberty to ask for healing with faith. It is to chasten them that the Lord permits Satan to inflict sickness on them, and by it keeps them chained and prisoners. God chastens us *"for our profit, that we may be partakers of his holiness,"* and that we may be sanctified, *"meet for the master's use."*

The discipline that the sickness inflicts brings great blessings with it. It is a call to the sick one to reflect; it leads him to see that God is occupied with him, and seeks to show him what there is that still separates him from the Master. God speaks to him, calling him to examine His ways, to acknowledge that he has lacked holiness, and that the purpose of the chastisement is to make him a partaker of His holiness. He awakens within him the desire to be enlightened by the Holy Spirit down to the inmost recesses of his heart, to get a clear idea of what his life has been up to the present time—a life of self-will, very unlike the holy life that God requires of him. He leads him to confess his sins, to entrust them to the Lord Jesus, to believe that the Savior can deliver him from them. He urges him to yield to Him, to consecrate his life to Him, to die to himself so that he may be able to live for God.

Sanctification is not something that you can accomplish yourself. It cannot even be produced by God in you as something that you can possess and contemplate yourself. No, it is the Holy Spirit, the Spirit of holiness alone, who can communicate His holiness to you and renew it continually. Therefore, it is by faith that you become partakers of His holiness. Jesus sanctifies you for God (1 Cor. 1:30), and the Holy Spirit imparts to you His holiness, which was manifested in His life on earth.

Surrender yourself to Him by faith, so that He may enable you to live that life from hour to hour. Believe that the Lord will, by His Spirit, lead you into, and keep you in, this life of holiness and of consecration to God's service. Live thus in the obedience of faith, always attentive to His voice and the guidance of His Spirit.

From the time that this fatherly discipline has led the sick one to a life of holiness, God has attained His purpose, and He will heal him who asks it in faith. Our earthly parents *"for a few days chastened us....No chastening seems to be joyful for the present, but painful; nevertheless, afterward it yields the peaceable fruit of righteousness to those who have been trained by it"* (Heb. 12:10–11 NKJV). Yes, it is when the believer realizes this *"peaceable fruit of righteousness"* that he is in a condition to be delivered from the chastisement.

Because believers still cannot understand that sanctification means an entire consecration to God, they cannot really believe that healing will quickly follow the sanctification of the sick one. Good health is too often for them only a matter of personal comfort and enjoyment that they may dispose of at their will. God cannot minister to this kind of selfishness. If they understood better that God requires His children to be *"sanctified, and meet for the master's use,"* they would not be surprised to see Him giving healing and renewed strength to those who have learned to place their entire bodies at His disposal, willing to be sanctified and employed in His service by the Holy Spirit. The Spirit of healing is also the Spirit of sanctification.

Thirteen

Sickness and Death

Surely he shall deliver thee from the snare of the fowler, and from the noisome pestilence....Thou shalt not be afraid for the terror by night; nor for the arrow that flieth by day; nor for the pestilence that walketh in darkness; nor for the destruction that wasteth at noonday....With long life will I satisfy him, and show him my salvation.
—Psalm 91:3, 5-6, 16

They shall still bring forth fruit in old age; they shall be fat and flourishing.
—Psalm 92:14

An objection is often made to the words of the apostle James, *"The prayer of faith shall save the sick"* (James 5:15), in this form: If we have the promise of being always healed in answer to prayer, how can it be possible to die? And some add, How can a sick person know whether God, who fixes the times of our lives, has not decided that we will die by such a sickness? In such a case, would not prayer be useless, and would it not be a sin to ask for healing?

Before replying, we would remark that this objection touches not only those who believe in Jesus as the Healer of the sick, but the Word of God itself, and the promise so clearly declared in the epistle of James and elsewhere. We are not at liberty to change or to limit the promises of God whenever they present some difficulty to us; neither can we insist that they be clearly explained to us before we bring ourselves to believe what they state. We begin by simply receiving them without resistance. Only then can the Spirit of God find us in the state of mind in which we can be taught and enlightened.

In the beginning, it will be difficult to completely understand a divine truth that has been neglected in the church for such a long time. It is only little by little that its importance and bearing are discerned. Gradually, as it revives, after it has been accepted by faith, the Holy Spirit will accompany it with new light. Let us remember that it is by the unbelief of the church that divine healing has left her. Faith in Bible truths should be made to depend on nothing but the Holy Spirit's enlightenment. *"There ariseth light in the darkness"* (Ps. 112:4) for the *"upright"* (v. 4)—for those who are ready to submit themselves to the Word of God.

It is easy to reply to the first objection. Scripture fixes seventy or eighty years as the ordinary measure of human life. The believer who receives Jesus as the Healer of the sick should be satisfied with this declaration of the Word of God. He will feel at liberty to *expect* a life of seventy or eighty years, but not necessarily longer. Besides, the man of faith places himself under the direction of the Spirit, which will enable him to discern the will of God regarding him, if something should prevent his attaining the age of seventy. Just as it is on earth, every rule in heaven has its exceptions.

We are sure according to the Word of God, whether by the words of Jesus or by those of James, that our heavenly Father wills to see His children in good health, so that they may labor in His service. For the same reason, He wills to set them free from sickness as soon as they have made a confession of sin and prayed with faith for their healing. For the believer who has walked with his Savior, full of the strength that comes from divine healing, and under the influence of the Holy Spirit, it is not necessary that when his time comes to die, he should die of sickness. The death of the believer, when the end of his life has come, is to fall asleep in Jesus Christ (1 Cor. 15:18). For him, death is only sleep after fatigue, the entering into rest.

The promise *"that it may be well with thee, and that thou mayest live long on the earth"* (Eph. 6:3) is addressed to us who live under the new covenant. The more the believer has learned to see the Savior as He who *"took our infirmities"* (Matt. 8:17), the more he has the liberty to claim the literal fulfillment of the promises: *"With long life will I satisfy him"*; *"They shall bring forth fruit in old age; they shall be fat and flourishing."*

The same text applies to the second objection. The sick one sees in God's Word that it is His will to heal His children after the confession of their sins, and in answer to the prayer of faith. It does not follow that they will be exempt from other trials. But as for sickness, they are healed of it because it attacks the body, which has become the dwelling place of the

61

Holy Spirit. The sick one should then desire healing, so that the power of God may be made manifest in him, and that he may serve Him in accomplishing His will. In this, he clings to the revealed will of God. As for that which is not yet revealed, he knows that God will make known His mind to His servants who walk with Him.

Remember that faith is not a logical reasoning that obliges God to act according to His promises. It is, rather, the confident attitude of a child who honors his Father and counts on His love. He knows His Father fulfills His promises and is faithful to communicate the new strength that flows from redemption to the body as well as to the soul, until the moment of departure comes.

Fourteen

The Holy Spirit—The Spirit of Healing

Now there are diversities of gifts, but the same Spirit....
To another faith by the same Spirit; to another
the gifts of healing by the same Spirit;...but all these
worketh that one and the selfsame Spirit,
dividing to every man severally as he will.
—1 Corinthians 12:4, 9, 11

What is it that distinguishes the children of God? What is their glory? It is that God dwells in the midst of them and reveals Himself to them in power (Exod. 33:16; 34:9–10). Under the new covenant, this dwelling of God in the believer is even more manifest than in former times. God sends the Holy Spirit to His church—the body of Christ—to act in her with power. Her life and her prosperity depend on Him. The Spirit must find unreserved, full liberty in her, so that she may be recognized as the church of Christ, the Lord's body. In every age, the church may look for manifestations of the Spirit, for they form our indissoluble unity: *"one body and one Spirit"* (Eph. 4:4).

Divine Healing

The Spirit operates in various members of the church at different times. It is possible to be filled with the Spirit for one special work and not for another. There are also times in the history of the church when certain gifts of the Spirit are given with power, while at the same time ignorance or unbelief may hinder other gifts. Wherever the more abundant life of the Spirit is to be found, we may expect Him to manifest all His gifts.

The gift of healing is one of the most beautiful manifestations of the Spirit. It is recorded of Jesus, *"God anointed Jesus of Nazareth...who went about doing good, and healing all that were oppressed of the devil"* (Acts 10:38). The Holy Spirit in Him was a healing Spirit, and He was the same in the disciples after Pentecost. Thus the words of our text express what was the continuous experience of the early churches. (See Acts 3:7; 4:30; 5:12, 15–16; 6:8; 8:7; 9:41; 14:9–10; 16:18–19; 19:12; 28:8–9.) The abundant outpouring of the Spirit produced abundant healings. What a lesson for the church in our day!

Divine healing is the work of the Holy Spirit. Christ's redemption extends its powerful working to the body, and the Holy Spirit is in charge of transmitting it to us and maintaining it in us. Our bodies share in the benefit of the redemption, and even now we can receive the pledge of it by divine healing. It is Jesus who heals, Jesus who anoints and baptizes with the Holy Spirit, and Jesus who baptized His disciples with the same Spirit. It is He who sends us the Holy Spirit here on earth to take sickness away from us and to restore us to health.

Divine healing accompanies the sanctification by the Spirit. It is to make us holy that the Holy Spirit makes us partakers of Christ's redemption. Hence His name "Holy." Therefore, the healing that He works is an intrinsic part of His divine mission. He bestows this healing to lead the sick one to be converted and to believe (Acts 4:29–30; 5:12, 14; 6:7–8; 8:6, 8; 9:42) or to confirm his faith if he is already converted. The Spirit constrains him thus to renounce sin and to consecrate himself entirely to God and to His service (1 Cor. 11:31; James 5:15–16; Heb. 12:10).

Divine healing glorifies Jesus. It is God's will that His Son should be glorified, and the Holy Spirit does this when He comes to show us what the redemption of Christ does for us. The redemption of the mortal body appears almost more marvelous than that of the immortal soul. In these two ways, God wills to dwell in us through Christ, and thus to triumph over the flesh. As soon as our bodies become the temple of God through the Spirit, Jesus is glorified.

Divine healing takes place wherever the Spirit of God works in power. Examples of this are to be found in the lives of the Reformers, and in other men of God called to His service over the centuries. But there are even more promises accompanying the outpouring of the Holy Spirit that have not been fulfilled up to this time. Let us live in a holy expectation, praying for the Lord to accomplish them in us.

Fifteen

Persevering Prayer

*And he spake a parable unto them to this end, that men
ought always to pray, and not to faint; saying, There was
in a city a judge, which feared not God, neither regarded
man: and there was a widow in that city; and she came
unto him, saying, Avenge me of mine adversary. And he
would not for a while: but afterward he said within
himself, Though I fear not God, nor regard man; yet because
this widow troubleth me, I will avenge her, lest by her
continual coming she weary me. And the Lord said, Hear
what the unjust judge saith. And shall not God avenge his
own elect, which cry day and night unto him, though he
bear long with them? I tell you that he will avenge them
speedily. Nevertheless when the Son of man cometh,
shall he find faith on the earth?*
—Luke 18:1–8

The necessity of praying with perseverance is the
secret of all spiritual life. What a blessing to be
able to ask the Lord for a particular answer until He
gives it, knowing with certainty that it is His will to
answer prayer! But what a mystery the call to persevere in prayer is for us—to knock in faith at His

door, to remind Him of His promises, and to do so without wearying until He grants us our petition! That our prayers can obtain from the Lord something He would not otherwise give should prove that man has been created in the image of God, that he is His friend, that he is His fellow worker. The believers who together form the body of Christ partake of His intercessory work in this manner. It is to Christ's intercession that the Father responds, and to which He grants His divine favors.

More than once the Bible explains to us the need for persevering prayer. There are many grounds for it, the chief of which is the justice of God. God has declared that sin must bear its consequences. Sin, therefore, has rights over a world that welcomes and remains enslaved by it. When the child of God seeks to quit this way of life, it is necessary that the justice of God consent to his request. Time is needed, however, for the privileges that Christ obtained for the believers to go into effect.

Besides this, the opposition of Satan, who always seeks to prevent the answer to prayer, is a reason for it (Dan. 10:12–13). The only means by which this unseen Enemy can be conquered is faith. Standing firmly on the promises of God, faith refuses to yield, continuing to pray and wait for the answer, even when it is delayed, knowing that the victory is sure (Eph. 6:12–13).

Finally, perseverance in prayer is necessary for ourselves. Delay in the answer is intended to prove and strengthen our faith. It ought to develop in us a steadfast faith that will no longer let go of the promises of God, but that renounces its own side of things to trust in God alone. It is then that God, seeing our faith, finds us ready to receive His favor and grants it to us. He will avenge speedily, even though He tarries. Yes, notwithstanding all the necessary delays, He will not make us wait a moment too long. If we cry to Him day and night, He will answer us speedily.

This perseverance in prayer will become easy for us, as soon as we fully understand what faith is. Jesus teaches us in these words: *"All things whatsoever ye shall ask in prayer, believing, ye shall receive"* (Matt. 21:22). When the Word of God authorizes us to ask for anything, we should believe that we receive it at once. God gives it to us; this we know by faith. We can say, between God and us, that we have received it, although it might be only later that we are permitted to realize the effects here on earth. Before having seen or experienced anything tangible, faith rejoices in having received, and perseveres in praying and waiting until the answer is manifested. Sometimes, it is useful to continue to pray, just to learn to count on the answer. After having believed that we are heard, it is good to persevere until it has become an accomplished fact.

This is of great importance in obtaining divine healing. Sometimes, it is true that healing is immediate and complete. But it may happen that we have to wait, even when a sick person has been able to ask for healing in faith. Sometimes, also, the first symptoms of healing are immediately obvious, but afterward, the following progress is slow and interrupted by times when it is arrested or when the evil returns. In either case, it is important, as much for the sick person as for those who pray with him, to believe in the effectiveness of persevering prayer, even though they may not understand the mystery of it. That which God appears at first to refuse, He grants later in response to the prayer of the woman from Canaan, to the prayer of the widow, and to that of the friend who knocks at midnight (Matt. 15:22–28; Luke 18:3–8; 11:5–8). Without regarding either change or answer, faith that is grounded on the Word of God, and that continues to pray with importunity, ends by gaining the victory. *"Shall not God avenge his own elect which cry day and night unto him, though he bear long with them? I tell you that he will avenge them speedily."*

God's timing is perfect. He can delay anything as He sees necessary, and then more speedily bring the answer at just the right moment. The same two abilities should belong to our faith. Let us grasp the grace that is promised to us, as if we had already received it, but wait with untiring patience for the answer that is slow to come. Such faith belongs to living in Him. It is in order to produce this faith in us that sickness is sent to us, and that healing is granted to us, for such faith, above all, glorifies God.

Sixteen

Let Him Who Is Healed
Glorify God

And immediately he received his sight,
and followed him, glorifying God and all the people,
when they saw it, gave praise unto God.
—Luke 18:43

And he leaping up stood, and walked,
and entered with them into the temple,
walking, and leaping, and praising God.
—Acts 3:8

It is a prevalent idea that piety is easier in sickness than in health, and that silent suffering inclines the soul to seek the Lord more than the distractions of active life. For these reasons, sick people sometimes hesitate to ask for healing from the Lord. They believe the sickness may be more of a blessing to them apiritually than health. To think in this way is to ignore that healing and its fruits are divine. Although healing by earthly remedies alone may cause God to relax His hand, divine healing, on the contrary, binds us more closely to Him. Thus in our day,

71

as in the time of the early ministry of Jesus Christ, the believer who has been healed by Him can glorify Him far better than the one who remains sick. Sickness can glorify God only insofar as it manifests His power. (See John 9:3; 11:4.)

The sufferer who is led by his sufferings to give glory to God does it, so to speak, by constraint. If he had health and the liberty to choose, it is quite possible that his heart would turn back to the world. In such a case, the Lord must keep him where he is; his piety depends on his sickly condition. This is why the world supposes that Christianity is hardly effective anywhere but in sick rooms or on deathbeds. In order for the world to be convinced of the power of faith against temptation, it must see the healthy believer walking in calmness and holiness, even in the midst of work and active life. Although many sick people may have glorified God by their patience in suffering, He can be more glorified still by a health that He has sanctified.

Why then, we are asked, should those who have been healed in answer to the prayer of faith glorify the Lord more than those who have been healed through earthly remedies alone? Here is the reason: Healing by means of remedies shows us the power of God in nature, but it does not bring us into living and direct contact with Him. Divine healing, however, is an act proceeding directly from God, relying on nothing but the Holy Spirit.

In this latter case, contact with God is what is essential, and it is for this reason that an examination of the conscience and the confession of sins should be the preparation for it (1 Cor. 11:30–32; James 5:15–16). One who is healed by divine intervention alone is called to consecrate himself anew and entirely to the Lord (1 Cor. 6:13, 19). All this depends on the act of faith that takes the Lord's promise, yields to Him, and never doubts that the Lord takes immediate possession of what is consecrated to Him. This is why the continuance of the health received depends on the holiness of the life of the believer, and the obedience to always seek the pleasure of the divine Healer (Exod. 15:26).

Health obtained under such conditions ensures spiritual blessings much greater than the mere restoration to health by ordinary means. When the Lord heals the body, it is so that He may take possession of it and make it a temple that He may dwell in. The joy that then fills the soul is indescribable. It is not only the joy of being healed, but it is also joy mingled with humility and a holy enthusiasm that realizes the touch of the Lord, receiving a new life from Him. In the exuberance of his joy, the healed one exalts the Lord, glorifies Him by word and deed, and consecrates all his life to God.

It is evident that these fruits of healing are not the same for everyone, and that sometimes backward steps are made. The life of the healed one joins with the life of believers around him. Their doubts and their inconsistencies may make his steps totter, although this generally results in a new beginning. Each day he discovers and recognizes afresh that his life is the Lord's life. He enters into a more intimate and more joyous communion with Him, learning to live in habitual dependence on Jesus and receiving from Him the strength that results from a more complete consecration.

Divine Healing

Oh, what the church can become when she lives in this faith! When every sick person recognizes in sickness a call to be holy, and *expects* a manifestation of the Lord's presence, then healings will be multiplied. Each will produce a witness of the power of God, all ready to cry with the psalmist, *"Bless the Lord, O my soul,...who healeth all thy diseases"* (Ps. 103:2–3).

Seventeen

The Need of a Manifestation of God's Power

And now, Lord, behold their threatenings: and grant
unto thy servants, that with all boldness they may
speak thy word, by stretching forth thine hand to heal,
and that signs and wonders may be done by the name
of thy holy child Jesus. And when they had prayed,
the place was shaken where they were assembled together;
and they were all filled with the Holy Ghost,
and they spake the word of God with boldness.
—Acts 4:29–31

Is it permissible to ask the Lord, *"Grant unto thy servants, that with all boldness they may speak thy word, by stretching forth thine hand to heal"*? Let us look into this question.

The Word of God meets as many difficulties in our day as then, and today's needs are equally pressing. Imagine the apostles in the midst of Jerusalem and her unbelief. The rulers of the people were making threats, while the blinded multitude were refusing to accept Jesus. The world is no longer as openly hostile to the church, because it has lost its fear of her, but its tolerance is more to be dreaded than its hatred. Apathy is sometimes worse than violence. A Christianity of mere form, in the sleep of indifference, is just as inaccessible as an openly resisting Judaism. Even in the present day, God's servants need His power to be clearly evident among them, so that the Word can be preached with all boldness.

The help of God is as necessary now as it was then. The apostles knew very well that it was not the eloquence of their preaching that caused the truth to triumph. They were aware of their dependence on the Holy Spirit manifesting His presence by miracles. It was necessary for the living God to stretch forth His hand, so that there might be healings, miracles, and signs in the name of His holy Son Jesus. Only then could His servants rejoice. Strengthened by His presence, they could then speak His Word with boldness and teach the world to fear His name.

The divine promises should concern us today, also. The apostles counted on these words of the Lord before He ascended: *"Go ye into all the world, and preach the gospel to every creature....And these signs shall follow them that believe;...they shall lay hands on the sick, and they shall recover"* (Mark 16:15, 17–18). This charge indicates the divine vocation of the church. The promise that follows shows us what her armor is and proves to us that the Lord acts in agreement with her. Because the apostles counted on this promise, they prayed for the Lord to grant them this proof of His presence. They had been filled with the Holy Spirit on the Day of Pentecost, but they still needed the supernatural signs that His power works.

The Need of a Manifestation of God's Power

The same promise is intended just as much for us. The command to preach the Gospel cannot be severed from the promise of divine healing with which it is accompanied. Nowhere is it found in the Bible that this promise was not for future times. In all ages, God's people greatly need to know that the Lord is with them and to possess the irrefutable proof of it. Therefore, this promise *is for us;* let us pray for its fulfillment.

Should we expect the same grace? We read in the book of Acts that when the apostles had prayed,

> *they were all filled with the Holy Ghost, and they spake the word of God with boldness.... And by the hands of the apostles were many signs and wonders wrought among the people...and believers were the more added to the Lord, multitudes both of men and women.* (Acts 4:31; 5:12, 14)

What joy and new strength God's people would receive today if the Lord would thus stretch forth His hand! Many tired and discouraged laborers grieve that they do not see more results from, and more blessings on, their labors. Their faith would be rejuvenated if signs of this kind would arise to prove that God is with them!

Many who are indifferent would be led to reflect, more than one doubter would regain confidence, and all unbelievers would be reduced to silence. The poor sinner would wake up if he saw with his own eyes what he could not comprehend by words only. He would be forced to acknowledge that the Christian's God is the living God who does wonders, the God of love who blesses!

Divine Healing

Awake and put on your strength, church of Christ. Although, because of your unfaithfulness, you have lost the joy of seeing your preaching of the Word allied with the hand of the Lord stretched out to heal, the Lord is ready to grant you this grace again. Acknowledge that it is your own unbelief that has so long deprived you of it, and pray for pardon. Clothe yourself with the strength of prayer.

"Awake, awake, put on strength, O arm of the LORD; awake, as in the ancient days" (Isa. 51:9).

Eighteen

Sin and Sickness

The prayer of faith shall save the sick, and the Lord
shall raise him up; and if he has committed sins, they
shall be forgiven him. Confess your faults one to another,
and pray one for another, that ye may be healed.
—James 5:15–16

Here, as in other Scriptures, the pardon of sins
and the healing of sickness are closely united.
James declared that a pardon of sins would be
granted with the healing. For this reason, he desired
to see confession of sin accompanying the prayer
that claims healing. We know that confession of sin
is necessary to obtain the pardon of sin from God. It
is equally necessary to obtain healing. Unconfessed
sin presents an obstacle to the prayer of faith. It
could even cause the sickness to reappear. When
called to treat a patient, a physician should first di-
agnose the cause of the disease. If he succeeds, he
stands a better chance of combating it. Our God also
goes back to the primary cause of all sickness—sin.
It is the patient's part to confess the sin, and it is
God's part to grant the pardon that removes this

first cause, so that healing can take place. When seeking healing by means of earthly remedies, find a clever physician and follow his prescriptions. When seeking healing through the prayer of faith, however, keep your eyes on the Lord, and be continuously conscious of how you stand with Him. James, therefore, was showing his readers a condition that was essential to the recovery of their health; namely, they must confess and forsake sin.

Sickness can be a consequence of sin. Often God permits sickness in order to show us our faults, chasten us, and purify us from them. Sickness is, I believe, a visible sign of God's judgment on sin. The one who is sick is not necessarily a greater sinner than another who is in health. On the contrary, it is often the holiest among the children of God whom He chastens, as we see from the example of Job. Sickness is also not always intended to check some fault that we can easily determine. Its main purpose is to draw the attention of the sick one to that which remains in him of the egotism of the *"old man"* (Rom. 6:6) and of all that hinders him from a life entirely consecrated to his God.

The first step that the sick one has to take in the path of divine healing will be, therefore, to let the Holy Spirit of God probe his heart and convict him of sin. This will be followed by humiliation, a decision to break with sin, and confession. To confess our sins is to lay them down before God and to subject them to His judgment, with the full intention of falling into them no more. A sincere confession will be followed by a new assurance of pardon.

"If he has committed sins, they shall be forgiven him." When we have confessed our sins, we must

receive the promised pardon, believing that God gives it. Faith in God's pardon is often vague for a young Christian. Either he is uncertain about its meaning, or he has difficulty accepting it. But if he receives the pardon with confidence, in answer to the prayer of faith, it will bring him new life and strength. His soul will rest in the redemption of the blood of Christ, receiving the certainty from the Holy Spirit of his pardon. Therefore, nothing remains to hinder the Savior from filling him with His love and with His grace. God's pardon brings with it a divine life that acts powerfully on him who receives it.

Once the soul has consented to make a sincere confession and has obtained pardon, it is ready to grasp God's promise of healing. Believing that the Lord will raise up His sick one is no longer difficult. It is when we keep far away from God that it is difficult to believe; confession and pardon bring us quite near to Him. As soon as the cause of the sickness has been removed, the sickness itself can be arrested. It now becomes easy for the sick one to believe that if the Lord subjected his body to the chastisement of sickness because of his sins, He now wills that this same body should be healed, because the sin is pardoned. His presence is revealed; a ray of life—of His divine life—comes to quicken the body; and the sick one proves that as soon as he is no longer separated from the Lord, the prayer of faith does save the sick.

Nineteen

Jesus Bore Our Sickness

Surely he hath borne our griefs, and carried our sorrows:
yet we did esteem him stricken, smitten of God,
and afflicted....He shall see of the travail of his soul,
and shall be satisfied: by his knowledge shall
my righteous servant justify many; for he shall bear
their iniquities. Therefore will I divide him a portion
with the great, and he shall divide the spoil with the
strong; because...he bare the sin of many.
—Isaiah 53:4, 11–12

Are you familiar with the beautiful fifty-third chapter of Isaiah, which has been called the fifth Gospel? Enlightened by the Spirit of God, Isaiah predicted the sufferings of the Lamb of God and described the divine grace that would result from them.

The words *to bear* had to appear in this prophecy. These words must accompany the mention of sin, whether as committed directly by the sinner, or as transmitted to a substitute. The transgressor, the priest, and the atoning victim must all bear the sin. In the same way, it is because the Lamb of God has borne our sins that God smote Him for the iniquity of us all. Sin was not found in Him, but it was put on Him; He took it voluntarily. It is because He bore it, and, in bearing it, put an end to it, that He has the power to save us. *"My righteous servant* [shall] *justify many, for he shall bear their iniquities....He shall divide the spoil with the strong; because...he bare the sin of many."* It is, therefore, because our sins have been borne by Jesus Christ that we are delivered from them as soon as we believe this truth; consequently, we no longer have to bear them ourselves.

In Isaiah 53, the verb *to bear* occurs twice, but in relation to two different things. It is said not only that the Lord's righteous Servant bore our sins (v. 12), but also that He bore our griefs, or sicknesses (v. 4). Thus His bearing our sicknesses as well as our sins forms an integral part of the Redeemer's work. Although He was without sin, He has borne our sins, and has done the same with our sicknesses.

The human part of Jesus could not be touched by sickness, because it remained holy. We never find in the account of His life any mention of sickness. Although experiencing all of our human weaknesses—hunger, thirst, fatigue, and sleep—because these things are not the consequence of sin, He still had no trace of sickness. Sickness had no hold on Him because He was without sin. He could, therefore, die only a violent death (and that only by His voluntary consent). Thus, it is not in Him, but *on Him* that we see sickness as well as sin. He took them on Himself and bore them of His own free will. By bearing them, He triumphed over them and has acquired the right of delivering His children from them.

Jesus Bore Our Sickness

Sin had attacked and ruined the soul and body equally. Jesus came to save both. Having taken sickness as well as sin on Himself, He is in a position to set us free from the one as well as the other. In order for Him to accomplish this double deliverance, He expects only one thing from us: our faith.

As soon as a sick believer understands the meaning of the words, "Jesus has borne my sins," he is not afraid to say, "I no longer need to bear my sins." In the same way, as soon as he fully believes that Jesus has borne our sicknesses, he is not afraid to say, "I no longer need to bear my sickness." Jesus, in bearing sin, bore sickness also. He has made payment for both, and He delivers us from both.

I witnessed the blessed influence this truth exercised one day. A sick woman had spent almost seven years in bed. A sufferer from tuberculosis, epilepsy, and other sicknesses, she had been assured that no hope of a cure remained for her. She was carried into the room where the late Mr. W. E. Boardman was holding a Sunday evening service for the sick, and was laid in a half-fainting condition on the sofa. She was too little conscious to remember anything of what took place until she heard the words, *"Himself took our infirmities and bare our sicknesses"* (Matt. 8:17). She then seemed to hear the words, "If He has borne your sicknesses, why then bear them yourself? Get up."

"But," she thought, "if I attempt to get up, and fall on the ground, what will they think of me?"

But the inward voice began again, "If He has borne my sins, why should I have to bear them?" To the astonishment of all who were present, she rose, and, although still feeble, sat down in a chair by the table. From that moment, her healing made rapid progress. At the end of a few weeks, she no longer had the appearance of an invalid. Soon she was so strong that she could spend many hours a day in visiting the poor. With what joy and love she could then speak of Him who was *the strength of* [her] *life"* (Ps. 27:1)! She had believed that Jesus had borne her sicknesses as well as her sins, and her faith remained firm. It is thus that Jesus reveals Himself as a perfect Savior to all those who will trust themselves unreservedly to Him.

Twenty

Is Sickness a Chastisement?

For this cause many are weak and sickly among you,
and many sleep. For if we would judge ourselves,
we should not be judged. But when we are judged,
we are chastened of the Lord, that we should
not be condemned with the world.
—1 Corinthians 11:30–32

In writing to the Corinthians, the apostle Paul had to reprove them for the manner in which they observed the Lord's Supper, which had caused them to be chastised by God. Here we see sickness as a judgment of God, a chastisement for sin. Paul saw it as such, and added that it was in order to prevent them from falling more deeply into sin—to prevent them from being *"condemned with the world"*—that they were thus afflicted. He warned them that if they would rather be neither judged nor chastened by the Lord, they should examine themselves to discover the cause of their sickness and condemn their own sins. The Lord would then no longer need to exercise severity. Is it not evident that in this instance sickness is a judgment of God, a chastisement of sin, that

87

we can avoid by examining and condemning ourselves?

Yes, sickness is (more often than we know) a chastisement for sin. God *"doth not afflict willingly nor grieve the children of men"* (Lam. 3:33). It is not without a cause that He allows us to be deprived of health. Perhaps it is to make us more aware of a particular sin from which we can repent. *"Sin no more, lest a worse thing come unto thee"* (John 5:14). Perhaps we have become entangled in pride and worldliness. Or it may be that self-confidence or caprice have entered our service for God.

It is, however, quite possible that the chastisement may not be directed against any particular sin. It may be the result of the sin that weighs upon the entire human race. In the case of the man born blind, the disciples asked the Lord, *"Who did sin, this man or his parents, that he was born blind?"* and He answered, *"Neither hath this man sinned nor his parents"* (John 9:3). He does not say that sin and sickness are not related, but He teaches us not to accuse every sick person of sin.

In any case, sickness is always a discipline that ought to awaken our attention to sin and turn us from it. Therefore, a sick person should begin by judging himself (1 Cor. 11:31), by placing himself before his heavenly Father with a sincere desire to see anything that could have grieved Him or could have rendered the chastisement necessary. In so doing, he may count assuredly on the Holy Spirit's light to clearly show him his failure.

Let him be ready to renounce at once what he may discern, and to place himself at the Lord's disposal to serve Him with perfect obedience.

Is Sickness a Chastisement?

But do not let him imagine that he can conquer sin by his own efforts. No, that is impossible for him. He can, however, with all his power of will, join God in renouncing the sin, and then believe that he is accepted by Him. In so doing, he will be yielding himself, consecrating himself anew to God, willing to do only His holy will in all things.

Scripture assures us that if we thus examine ourselves, the Lord will not judge us. Our Father chastens His children only as far as it is necessary. God seeks to deliver us from sin and self. As soon as we understand Him and break with these, sickness may cease; it has done its work.

We must find out what the sickness means, and recognize it as a part of the discipline of God. One may recognize vaguely that he commits sins, without attempting to define them. Even if he does, he may not believe it is possible to give them up. And if he goes so far as to renounce them, he may fail to count on God to put an end to the chastisement, despite the glorious assurance that Paul's words give us.

Dear sick one, have you considered that your heavenly Father may disapprove of some hidden sin in your life? He would like your sickness to help you discover it, and His Holy Spirit will guide you in the search. Renounce what He may point out to you at once. Then not even the smallest shadow will remain between your Father and you. It is His will to pardon your sin and to heal your sickness.

In Jesus, we have both pardon and healing; they are two sides of His redemptive work. He is calling you to live a life of dependence on Him in a greater degree than you have before. Abandon yourself to Him in complete obedience, and follow His steps like a little child. With joy, your heavenly Father will deliver you from chastisement. He will reveal Himself to you as your Healer, bringing you nearer to Him by this new tie of His love. He will make you obedient and faithful in serving Him. If, as a wise and faithful Father, He has been obliged to chasten you, it is also as a Father that He wills your healing, and that He desires to bless and keep you henceforth.

Twenty-one

God's Prescription for the Sick

Is any sick among you? let him call for the elders of the church; and let them pray over him, anointing him with oil in the name of the Lord: and the prayer of faith shall save the sick, and the Lord shall raise him up; and if he have committed sins, they shall be forgiven him.
—James 5:14–15

J ames 5:14–15, above all other Scriptures, most clearly declares to the sick what they have to do in order to be healed. Sickness and its consequences abound in the world. What joy, then, for the believer to learn from the Word of God the way of healing for the sick! The Bible teaches us that it is the will of God to see His children in good health. The apostle James had no hesitation in saying that *"the prayer of faith shall save the sick, and the Lord shall raise him up."* May the Lord teach us to pay attention to and receive with simplicity what His Word tells us!

Notice, first, that James made a distinction between affliction, or suffering, and sickness. In the previous verse, he said, *"Is any among you afflicted? let him pray"* (v. 13). He did not specify what we should request in such a case; he definitely did not say to ask for deliverance from suffering. No, suffering that may arise from various exterior causes is the portion of every Christian. Let us therefore understand that James' objective was to lead the tried believer to ask for deliverance only with a spirit of submission to the will of God, and, above all, to ask also for the patience that he considered to be the privilege of the believer (James 1:2–4, 12; 5:7–8).

But in dealing with the words, *"Is any sick among you?"* James replied in quite another manner. He said with assurance that the sick one may ask for healing with confidence that he will obtain it, and the Lord will hear him. There is, therefore, a great difference between suffering and sickness. The Lord Jesus spoke of suffering as being necessary, as being willed and blessed by God, while He said that sickness ought to be cured. All other suffering comes to us from without, and will cease only when Jesus triumphs over the sin and evil that are in the world. Sickness is an evil that is in the body itself, in this body saved by Christ, so that it may become the temple of the Holy Spirit. This body should, in my opinion, be healed as soon as the sick believer receives, by faith, the working of the Holy Spirit, the very life of Jesus in him.

What course did James instruct the sick to follow? Let him call for the elders of the church, and let the elders pray for him. In the time of James, there were physicians, but he did not tell the sick believer to turn to them. The elders then were the pastors and leaders of the churches, called to the ministry not because they had passed through schools of theology, but because they were filled with the Holy

Spirit, and were well-known for their piety and faith. Why should their presence be needed by the sick one? Couldn't he pray for himself? Couldn't his friends have prayed? Yes, but it is not so easy for everybody to exercise the faith that obtains healing. That is, without a doubt, one reason why James desired that men should be called whose faith was firm and sure.

Besides this, the elders were representatives of the church, of the collective body of Christ, for it is the communion of believers that invites the Spirit to act with power. In short, they should, after the pattern of the great Shepherd of the sheep, care for the flock as He does. They should identify themselves with the sick one, understand his trouble, receive from God the necessary discernment to instruct him, and encourage him to persevere in faith. It is, then, to the elders of the church that the healing of the sick is committed. And it is they, the servants of the God who pardons iniquities and heals diseases (Ps. 103:3), who are called to transmit to others the Lord's graces for soul and body.

Finally, there is a promise still more direct: that of healing. The apostle spoke of it as the certain consequence of the prayer of faith. *"The prayer of faith shall save the sick, and the Lord shall raise him up."* This promise ought to stimulate in every believer the desire and expectation of healing. As we receive these words with simplicity and as they are written, shouldn't we see in them an unlimited promise that offers healing to whoever will pray in faith? May the Lord teach us to study His Word with the faith of a truly believing heart!

Twenty-two

"The Lord That Healeth Thee"

*I will put none of these diseases upon thee
which I have brought upon the Egyptians,
for I am the LORD that healeth thee.*
—Exodus 15:26

How often have we read these words without daring to take them for ourselves, and without expectation that the Lord would fulfill them in us! We have seen in them that the people of God ought to be exempt from the diseases inflicted upon the Egyptians. But we believed that this promise applied only to the Old Testament, and that, by the direct intervention of the Lord, we who live under the New Testament cannot expect to be kept from, or healed of, sickness. Because we were obliged to recognize the superiority of the new covenant, we came, in our ignorance, to assert that sickness often brings great blessings. Consequently, we believed God had done well to withdraw what He had formerly promised, and to be no longer for us what He was for Israel, *"the LORD that healeth thee."*

But in our day, we see the church awakening and acknowledging her mistake. She sees that it is under the new covenant that the Lord Jesus acquired the title of Healer by all His miraculous healings. She is beginning to see that in charging His church to preach the Gospel to every creature, He has promised to be with her *"alway, even unto the end of the world"* (Matt. 28:20).

As the proof of His presence, His disciples should have the power to lay hands on the sick, who should then be healed (Mark 16:15–18). In the days of Pentecost, the miraculous outpouring of the Holy Spirit was accompanied by miraculous healings, which were evidence of the blessings brought about by the power from on high (Acts 3:16; 5:12; 9:40). There is nothing in the Bible to make the church believe that the promise made to Israel has since been retracted, and she hears, from the mouth of the apostle James, this new promise: *"The prayer of faith shall save* [or heal] *the sick"* (James 5:15).

The church knows that unbelief has always limited (or set boundaries around) the Holy One of Israel (Ps. 78:41), and she asks herself if it is not this same unbelief that is hindering the manifestation of God's power to heal today. Who can doubt it? It is not God or His Word that are to blame here; it is our unbelief that impedes the miraculous power of the Lord and that holds Him back from healing as He did in the past.

Let our faith awaken. Let it recognize and adore in Christ the full power in Him who says, *"I am the LORD that healeth thee."* It is by the works of God that we can best understand what His Word tells us. The healings that, again, are responding to the prayer of faith confirm, by gloriously illustrating, the truth of His promise.

Let us learn to see, in the risen Jesus, the divine Healer, and let us receive Him as such. In order that I may recognize, in Jesus, my justification, my strength, and my wisdom, I must grasp, by faith, that He really is all these things to me. When the Bible tells me that Jesus is the sovereign Healer, I must take hold of this truth and say, "Yes, Lord, it is You who are my Healer."

And why may I hold Him as such? Because He gives Himself to me, making me *"planted together"* (Rom. 6:5) with Him. Inseparably united to Him, I thus possess His healing power. His love is pleased to bestow His favors on His beloved, to communicate Himself with all His heart to all who desire to receive Him. Let us believe that He is ready to extend the treasure of blessing, contained in the name, *"The LORD that healeth thee,"* to all who know and who can trust in this divine name. This is the treatment for the sick indicated by the law of His kingdom.

When I bring my sickness to the Lord, I do not depend on what I see, what I feel, or what I think, but on what He says. Even when everything appears contrary to the expected healing, even if it should not take place at the time or in the way that I had thought I should receive it, even when the symptoms seem only to be aggravated, my faith, strengthened by the very waiting, should cling immovably to this word that has gone out of the mouth of God: *"I am the LORD that healeth thee."*

God is always seeking to make us true believers. Healing and health are of little value if they do not glorify God and serve to unite us more closely with

Him. Thus, in the matter of healing, our faith must always be put to the test. He who counts on the name of his God, who can hear Jesus saying to him, *"Said I not unto thee that if thou wouldest believe thou shouldest see the glory of God?"* (John 11:40), will have the joy of receiving from God Himself the healing of the body, and of seeing it take place in a manner worthy of God, conformable to His promises. When we read these words, *"I am the LORD that healeth thee,"* let us not fear to answer eagerly, "Yes, Lord, You are the Lord who heals me."

Twenty-three

Jesus Heals the Sick

He...healed all that were sick: that it might be fulfilled
which was spoken by Esaias the prophet, saying, Himself
took our infirmities, and bare our sickness.
—Matthew 8:16–17

I n a preceding chapter, we studied the words of the
prophet Isaiah. If you still have any doubt as to
the interpretation that has been given, I remind you
of what the Holy Spirit caused the evangelist Matthew to write. It is expressly said, regarding all the
sick ones whom Jesus healed, *"That it might be ful-*
filled which was spoken by Esaias the prophet." It
was because Jesus had taken our sickness on Himself that He could, that He ought to, heal them. If He
had not done so, one part of His work of redemption
would have remained powerless and fruitless.

The text of the Word of God is not generally understood in this way. It is the generally accepted
view that the miraculous healings done by the Lord
Jesus are to be considered only as the proof of His
mercy, or as being the symbol of spiritual graces.
They are not seen to be a necessary consequence of

redemption, although that is what the Bible declares. The body and the soul have been created to serve together as a habitation of God. The sickly condition of the body, as well as that of the soul, is a consequence of sin, and that is what Jesus came to bear, to atone for, and to conquer.

When the Lord Jesus was on earth, it was not in the character of the Son of God that He cured the sick, but as the Mediator who bore our sickness. This enables us to understand why Jesus gave so much time to His healing work, and why, also, the Bible evangelists speak of it in a manner so detailed.

Read, for example, what Matthew said about it:

Jesus went about all Galilee, teaching in their synagogues, and preaching the gospel of the kingdom, and healing all manner of sickness, and all manner of disease among the people. And his fame went throughout all Syria; and they brought unto him all sick people that were taken with divers diseases and torments, and those which were possessed with devils, and those which were lunatics, and those that had the palsy; and he healed them. (Matt. 4:23–24)

And Jesus went about all the cities and villages, teaching in their synagogues, and preaching the gospel of the kingdom, and healing every sickness and every disease among the people. (Matt. 9:35)

And when he had called unto him his twelve disciples, he gave them power against unclean

spirits, to cast them out, and to heal all manner of sickness, and all manner of disease.
(Matt. 10:1)

Still in the gospel of Matthew, when the disciples of John the Baptist came to ask Jesus if He was the Messiah, so that He might prove it to them, He replied, *"The blind receive their sight, and the lame walk, the lepers are cleansed, and the deaf hear, the dead are raised up, and the poor have the gospel preached to them"* (Matt. 11:5). After the cure of the withered hand, and the opposition of the Pharisees who sought to destroy Him, we read that *"great multitudes followed him, and he healed them all"* (Matt. 12:15). Later, the crowd followed Him into a desert place, *"and Jesus went forth and saw a great multitude, and was moved with compassion toward them, and he healed their sick"* (Matt. 14:14).

Further on in the passage we read,

They sent out into all that country round about, and brought unto him all that were diseased; and besought him that they might only touch the hem of his garment; and as many as touched were made perfectly whole.
(Matt. 14:35–36)

It is said, also, of the sick who were among the multitudes that they *"cast them down at Jesus' feet; and he healed them"* (Matt. 15:30). Matthew added, *"Insomuch that the multitude wondered, when they saw the dumb to speak, the maimed to be whole, the lame to walk, and the blind to see: and they glorified the God of Israel"* (v. 31). Finally, when He came into the coasts of Judea beyond Jordan, *"Great multitudes followed him, and he healed them there"* (Matt. 19:2).

Let us add to these various texts those that give us in detail the account of healings worked by Jesus. These healings give us not only the proof of His power during His life here on earth, but also the continual result of His work of mercy and of love, the manifestation of His power of redemption, which delivers the soul and body from the dominion of sin.

Yes, that was in very deed the purpose of God. If, then, Jesus bore our sicknesses as an integral part of the redemption, if He has healed the sick *"that it might be fulfilled which was spoken by Esaias,"* and if His Savior-heart is always full of mercy and of love, we can believe with certainty that to this very day it is the will of Jesus to heal the sick in answer to the prayer of faith.

Twenty-four

Fervent and Effectual Prayer

Pray one for another, that ye may be healed.
The effectual fervent prayer of a righteous man availeth
much. Elijah was a man subject to like passions as we are,
and he prayed earnestly that it might not rain:
and it rained not on the earth by the space of three years
and six months. And he prayed again: and the heaven
gave rain, and the earth brought forth her fruit.
—James 5:16–18

James knew that a faith that obtains healing is not the fruit of human nature; therefore, he added that the prayer must be *"fervent."* Only such prayer can be effective. In this James stood on the example of Elijah, a man of the same nature (subject to similar passions) as we are, drawing the inference that our prayer can and ought to be of the same nature as his. How, then, did Elijah pray? This will throw some light on what the prayer of faith should be.

Elijah received from God the promise that rain was about to fall on the earth (1 Kings 18:1), and he declared this to Ahab. Strong in the promise of his God, he went atop Mount Carmel to pray (v. 42;

James 5:18). He knew—he believed—that God's will was to send rain. Nevertheless, he had to pray, or the rain would not come. His prayer was no empty form; it was a real power, which was about to make itself felt in heaven. God willed that it would rain, but the rain would come only at Elijah's request, a request repeated with faith and perseverance until the appearance of the first cloud in the sky.

In order for the will of God to be accomplished, this will must, on one side, be expressed by a promise, and, on the other, be received and grasped by the believer who prays. He, therefore, must persevere in prayer to show God that his faith expects an answer, that it will not grow weary until it is obtained.

This is how prayer must be made for the sick. The promise of God, *"The Lord will raise him up"* (James 5:15), must be rested on, and His will to heal recognized. Jesus Himself teaches us to pray with faith that counts on the answer of God. He says to us, *"Whatever things you ask when you pray, believe that you receive them, and you will have them"* (Mark 11:24 NKJV). After the prayer of faith, which receives what God has promised before it manifests itself, comes the prayer of perseverance, which does not lose sight of what has been asked until God has fulfilled His promise (1 Kings 18:43).

There may be some obstacle that hinders the fulfillment of the promise, whether on the side of God and His righteousness (Deut. 9:18), or on the side of Satan and his constant opposition to the plans of God. This obstacle may still impede the answer to the prayer (Dan. 10:12–13). It may be also that our faith is called to persevere until the answer comes. He who prays six times fervently and stops there, when he ought to have prayed seven times (2 Kings 13:18–19), deprives himself of the answer to his prayer.

Perseverance in prayer, a perseverance that strengthens the faith of the believer against everything that may seem opposed to the answer, is a real miracle. It is one of the impenetrable mysteries of the life of faith. Does it not say to us that the Savior's redeemed one is indeed His friend, a member of His body, and that the government of the world and the gifts of divine grace depend in some sense on his prayers? Prayer, therefore, is no vain form. It is the work of the Holy Spirit, who intercedes here on earth in us and by us. As such, it is as powerful and as indispensable as the work of the Son interceding for us before the throne of God.

It might seem strange that after having prayed with the certainty of being heard, and having seen therein the will of God, we would still need to continue in prayer. Nevertheless, it is so. In Gethsemane, Jesus prayed three times in succession. On Mount Carmel, Elijah prayed seven times. And we, if we believe the promise of God without doubting, will pray until we receive the answer. Both the importunate friend at midnight (Luke 11:5–8) and the widow who beseiged the unjust judge (Luke 18:2–7) are examples of perseverance in seeking the end in view.

Let us learn from Elijah's prayer to humble ourselves and to recognize why the power of God cannot be manifested more in the church, whether in the healing of the sick, or in conversion, or sanctification. *"Ye have not because ye ask not"* (James 4:2). It also teaches us patience. In the cases where healing is delayed, let us remember that obstacles may exist over which only perseverance in prayer can triumph. Faith that ceases to pray, or that is allowed to relax in its fervor, cannot take hold of what God has nevertheless given. Do not let your faith in the promises of Scripture be shaken by those things that are as yet beyond your reach. God's promise remains the same: *"The prayer of faith shall save the sick"* (James 5:15).

May the prayer of Elijah strengthen our faith. Let us remember that we have to imitate them who through faith and patience inherit the promises (Heb. 6:12). If we learn to persevere in prayer, its fruit will be always more abundant, always more evident. We will obtain, as Jesus obtained when He was on earth, healing of the sick, often immediate healing, which will bring glory to God.

Twenty-five

Intercessory Prayer

*Confess your faults one to another, and pray one for
another, that ye may be healed. The effectual
fervent prayer of a righteous man availeth much.*
—James 5:16

J ames began by speaking of the prayers of the elders of the church; but here, he addressed all believers as he said, *"Pray one for another that ye may
be healed."* Having already spoken of confession and
of pardon, he added, *"Confess your faults one to another."*

This shows us that the prayer of faith that asks
for healing is not the prayer of one isolated believer,
but that it ought to unite the members of the body of
Christ in the communion of the Spirit. God certainly
hears the prayers of each one of His children as soon
as they are presented to Him with living faith, but
the sick one does not always possess such faith as
this. In order for the Holy Spirit to act with power,
there must be a union of several members of the
body of Christ unitedly claiming His presence. We
need one as well as the other.

This dependence on our fellow believers should be exercised in two ways. First of all, we must confess our faults to any whom we may have wronged and receive pardon from them. But besides this, one who is sick may see the cause of his sickness in a sin that he has committed and recognize it as a chastening of God. In such a case, he should acknowledge his sin before the elders, or brethren in Christ, who pray for him. This confession will enable them to pray with more light and more faith. Such confession will also be a touchstone that tests the sincerity of his repentance, for it is easier to confess our sins to God than to man. Before a man confesses, his humiliation needs to be real and his repentance sincere. The result will be a closer communion between the sick one and those who intercede for him, and their faith will be quickened anew.

"Pray one for another, that ye may be healed." Doesn't this clearly answer that frequently asked question: What is the use in going to miracle-working evangelists in faraway places? Doesn't the Lord hear prayer in whatever place it is offered? Yes, without any doubt, wherever a prayer in living faith rises up to God, it finds Him ready to grant healing. But the church has so neglected to believe in this truth that it is a rare thing in the present day to find Christians capable of praying in this manner.

Thus, we cannot be too grateful to the Lord that He has inspired certain believers with the desire to consecrate their lives, in part, to testify to the truth of divine healing. Their words and their faith awaken faith in the hearts of many sick ones who, without their help, would never arrive at it. These are the very people who always say to everybody,

"The Lord is to be found everywhere." Let Christians learn not to neglect the least part of the marvelous power of their God, and He will be able to manifest to all that He is always *"the LORD that healeth thee"* (Exod. 15:26). Let us take heed to obey the Word of God, to confess to one another, and to pray for one another that we may be healed.

James noted still another essential condition to successful prayer: it must be the prayer of the righteous. *"The effectual fervent prayer of a righteous man availeth much."* The Scriptures tell us that *"he that doeth righteousness is righteous, even as he* [Jesus] *is righteous"* (1 John 3:7). James himself was surnamed "The Just" because of his piety and the tenderness of his conscience. Whether one is an elder or a simple believer, only after he is wholly surrendered to God and living in obedience to His will can he pray effectively for the brethren.

John said as much: *"Whatsoever we ask, we receive of him, because we keep his commandments, and do those things which are pleasing in his sight"* (v. 22). It is, therefore, the prayer of one who lives in intimate communion with God that *"availeth much."* It is to such prayer that God will grant the answer that He would not be able to give to His children who do not live as close to Him.

We often hear these words quoted: *"The effectual fervent prayer of a righteous man availeth much,"* but very rarely is this passage taken in connection with its context or remembered that it is divine healing in particular that is in question here. May the Lord raise up in His church many of these righteous men, animated with living faith, whom He can use to glorify Jesus as the divine Healer of the sick!

Twenty-six

The Will of God

Thy will be done.
—Matthew 6:10

If the Lord will.
—James 4:15

In days of sickness, when doctors and medicines fail, recourse is generally taken to such Scriptures as, *"Thy will be done"* and *"If the Lord will."* They may easily become a stumbling block in the way of divine healing. How can I know, it is asked, whether or not it is God's will that I remain ill? And as long as this is an open question, how can I pray for a healing with faith?

Here, truth and error seem to touch. It is, indeed, impossible to pray with faith when we are not sure that we are asking according to the will of God. "I can," one may say, "pray fervently in asking God to do the best for me, believing that He will cure me if it is possible." As long as one prays thus, one is praying with submission, but it is not the prayer of faith. That is possible only when we are certain that we are asking according to the will of God. The question then resolves itself into how we can know what the will of God is. It is a great mistake to think that the child of God cannot know His will about healing.

In order to know His divine will, we must be guided by the Word of God. It is His Word that promises us healing. The promise of James 5 is so absolute that it is impossible to deny it. This promise only confirms other passages, equally strong, that tell us that Jesus Christ has obtained for us the healing of our diseases, because He has borne our sicknesses. According to this promise, we have the right to healing, because it is a part of the salvation that we have in Christ. Therefore, we may expect it with certainty. The Scriptures tell us that sickness is, in God's hands, the means of chastening His children for their sins, but that this discipline ceases to be exercised as soon as His suffering child acknowledges and turns from the sin. Isn't it just as clear to say that God desires to make use of sickness only to bring back His children when they are straying?

Sick Christian, open your Bible, study it, and see in its pages that sickness is a warning to renounce sin. Whoever acknowledges and forsakes his sins finds pardon and healing in Jesus. Such is God's promise in His Word. If the Lord had some other arrangement in mind for His children whom He was about to call home to Him, He would make His will known to them. By the Holy Spirit, He would give them a desire to depart. In other special cases, He would awaken some special conviction. As a general rule, however, the Word of God promises us healing in answer to the prayer of faith.

The Will of God

"Nevertheless," some might say, "is it not better in all things to leave it to the will of God?" They refer to those Christians who would have forced the hand of God with their prayers had they not added, "Thy will be done." Without that addition, they certainly would not have experienced blessing in the answer to their prayers. And these would say, "How do we know whether sickness would not be better for us than health?"

To begin with, this is no case of "forcing the hand of God," since it is His Word that tells us that it is His will to heal us. *The prayer of faith shall save the sick"* (James 5:15). God wills that the health of the soul should have a blessed influence on the health of the body, that the presence of Jesus in the soul should have its confirmation in the good condition of the body. And when you know that this is His will, you cannot say truthfully that you are leaving all things to Him. It is not leaving it to Him when you make use of all possible remedies to be healed, instead of resting on His promise. Your submission is nothing else than spiritual sloth in view of what God commands you to do.

As to knowing whether sickness is better than health, we do not hesitate to reply that the return to health, which is the fruit of giving up sin, of consecration to God, and of an ultimate communion with God, is infinitely better than sickness. *This is the will of God, even your sanctification"* (1 Thess. 4:3), and it is by healing that God confirms the reality of this. When Jesus comes to take possession of our bodies, and cures them miraculously, it follows that the health received must be maintained from day to day by an uninterrupted communion with Him. This experience of the Savior's power and love comes as a result that is far superior to any that sickness has to offer. Undoubtedly, sickness may teach us submission, but healing received directly from God makes us better acquainted with our Lord and teaches us to confide in Him more deeply. Besides, it prepares the believer to accomplish the service of God in a far better way.

Sick Christian, if you would really seek to know what the will of God is in this thing, do not let yourself be influenced by the opinions of others, nor by your own former prejudices, but listen to and study what the Word of God has to say. Examine whether it does indeed tell you that divine healing is a part of the redemption of Jesus, and that God wills that every believer should have the right to claim it. See whether it promises that the prayer of every child of God for healing will be heard, and whether health restored by the power of the Holy Spirit manifests the glory of God in the eyes of the church and of the world. Ask these things of the Word; it will answer you. According to the will of God, sickness is a discipline occasioned by sin (or shortcoming), and healing, granted to the prayer of faith, bears witness to His grace that pardons, that sanctifies, and that takes away sin.

Twenty-seven

Obedience and Health

There he made for them a statute and an ordinance, and there he proved them, and said, If thou wilt diligently hearken to the voice of the LORD thy God, and will do that which is right in his sight, and will give ear to his commandments, and keep all his statutes, I will put none of these diseases upon thee, which I have brought upon the Egyptians: for I am the LORD that healeth thee.
—Exodus 15:25–26

Israel was just released from the yoke of Egypt when their faith was put to the test in the desert by the waters of Marah. It was after the Lord had sweetened the bitter waters that He promised He would not put on the children of Israel any of the diseases that He had brought upon the Egyptians, as long as the Israelites would obey Him. They would be exposed to other trials. They might sometimes suffer the need of bread and of water, or they would have to contend with mighty foes and encounter great dangers. All these things might come upon them in spite of their obedience, but sickness would not touch them. In a world still under the power of

Satan, they might be a target for attacks coming from without, but their bodies would not be oppressed with sickness, for God had delivered them from it. Had He not said, *"If thou wilt diligently hearken to the voice of the LORD thy God...I will put none of these diseases upon thee, which I have brought upon the Egyptians: for I am the LORD that healeth thee"*? Elsewhere He said, *"Ye shall serve the LORD your God,...and I will take sickness away from the midst of thee"* (Exod. 23:25). (See also Leviticus 7:12–16; 26:14–16; 28:15–61.)

This calls our attention to a truth of the greatest importance: the intimate relationship that exists between obedience and health; and between sanctification, which is the health of the soul, and divine healing, which ensures the health of the body. Both are comprised in the salvation that comes from God. It is noteworthy that in several languages these three words—*salvation, healing,* and *sanctification*—are derived from the same root and present the same fundamental thought. (For instance, the German *heil,* salvation; *heilung,* healing; *heilichung,* sanctification.) Salvation is the redemption that the Savior has obtained for us; health is the salvation of the body, which also comes to us from the divine Healer; and, sanctification reminds us that true salvation and true health consist in being holy as God is holy. Thus it is in giving health to the body and sanctification to the soul that Jesus is really the Savior of His people. Our text clearly declares the relationship that exists between holiness of life and the healing of the body. The expressions that bear this out seem to be purposely multiplied: *"If thou wilt diligently hearken...and will do that which is right...and will give ear...and keep all his statutes, I will put none of these diseases upon thee."*

Here we have the key to all true obedience and holiness. We often think we know the will of God well as it is revealed in His Word, but why doesn't this knowledge inspire obedience? It is because in order to obey, we must begin by listening. *"If thou wilt diligently hearken to the voice of the Lord thy God...and give ear...."* As long as the will of God reaches me through the voice of a man, or through the reading of a book, it will have little power with me. But if I enter into direct communion with God and listen to His voice, His commandment is quickened with living power to accomplish its purpose.

Christ is the living Word, and the Holy Spirit is His voice. Listening to His voice means to renounce all our own will and wisdom, to close the ear to every other voice so as to expect no other direction but that of the Holy Spirit. One who is redeemed is like a servant or child who needs to be directed; he knows that he belongs entirely to God, and that all his being—spirit, soul, and body—ought to glorify God.

But he is equally conscious that this is above his strength, and that he needs to receive, hour by hour, the direction he needs. He knows, also, that the divine commandment, as long as it is a dead letter to him, cannot impart to him strength and wisdom, and that it is only as he attentively gives ear that he will obtain the desired strength. Therefore, he listens and learns to observe the laws of God. This life of attention and action, of renouncement and of crucifixion, constitutes a holy life. The Lord first brings it to us in the form of sickness, making us understand what we are lacking. He then shows us by our healing, which calls the soul to a life of continual attention to the voice of God.

Most Christians see nothing more in divine healing than a temporal blessing for the body, while in the promise of our holy God, its end is to make us holy. The call to holiness sounds stronger and clearer daily in the church. More and more believers are coming to understand that God wants them to be like Christ. The Lord is beginning, again, to make use of His healing virtue, seeking thereby to show us that, in our own day, the Holy One of Israel is still *"the LORD that healeth thee,"* and that it is His will to keep His people both in health of body and in obedience.

Let him who looks for healing from the Lord receive it with joy. It is not a legal obedience that is required of him, an obedience depending on his own strength. No, God asks of him, on the contrary, the abandonment of a little child, the attention that listens and consents to be led. This is what God expects of him. The healing of the body will respond to this childlike faith. The Lord will reveal Himself to him as the mighty Savior who heals the body and sanctifies the soul.

Twenty-eight

Job's Sickness and Healing

So went Satan forth from the presence of the Lord,
and smote Job with sore boils from the sole of his foot
unto his crown.
—Job 2:7

The veil that hides the unseen world from us is lifted for a moment in the mysterious history of Job, revealing heaven and hell occupied with God's servants on earth. We see in it the temptations peculiar to sickness, and how Satan makes use of them to dispute with God, and to seek the perdition of the soul of man. God, on the other hand, seeks to sanctify it by the very same trial. In the case of Job, we see, in God's light, where sickness comes from, what result it should have, and how it is possible to be delivered from it.

Where does sickness come from—from God or from Satan? Opinions on this point differ vastly. Some hold that it is sent from God; others see it as the work of the Wicked One. Both are in error, as long as they hold their view to the exclusion of that held by the other party, while both are in the right if they admit that there are two sides to this question. Let us say, then, that sickness comes from Satan, but that it cannot exist without the permission of God. On the other hand, the power of Satan is that of an oppressor, who has no right to attack man, but whose claims on man are legitimate in that God decrees that he who yields himself to Satan places himself under his domination.

Satan is the prince of the kingdom of darkness and of sin; sickness is the consequence of sin. This constitutes the right of Satan over the body of sinful man. He is the prince of this world, so recognized by God, until such time as he shall be legally conquered and dethroned. Consequently, he has a certain power over all those who remain down here under his jurisdiction. He then torments men with sickness and seeks thereby to turn them from God and to work their ruin.

But, we would hasten to say, the power of Satan is far from being almighty; it can do nothing without God's authorization. God permits him to do everything he does in tempting men, even believers, but it is in order that the trial may bring forth in them the fruit of holiness. It is also said that Satan has the power of death (Heb. 2:14), that he is everywhere that death reigns. Nevertheless, he has no power to decide as to the death of God's servants without the express will of God. It is the same with sickness. Because of sin, sickness is the work of Satan. But since supreme direction of this world belongs to God, it can also be regarded as the work of God. All who are acquainted with the book of Job know how very clearly this point is brought out there.

Job's Sickness and Healing

What should result from sickness? The result will be good or evil, depending on whether God or Satan has the victory in us. Under Satan's influence, a sick person sinks always deeper into sin. He does not recognize sin to be the cause of the chastisement, and he occupies himself exclusively with himself and with his suffering. He desires nothing but to be healed, without dreaming of a desire for deliverance from sin.

But wherever God gains the victory, sickness leads the sufferer to renounce himself and to abandon himself to God. The history of Job illustrates this. His friends accused him, unjustly, of having committed sins of exceptional gravity, which caused his terrible suffering. This was, however, not the case, since God Himself had borne him witness that he was *"perfect and upright, one that feared God and eschewed evil"* (Job 2:3).

But in defending himself, Job went too far. Instead of humbling himself in abasement before the Lord, and recognizing his hidden sins, he attempted in all self-righteousness to justify himself. It was not until the Lord appeared to him that he came to say, *"I abhor myself, and repent in dust and ashes"* (Job 42:6). To him, sickness became a "signal" blessing in bringing him to know God in quite a new way, and to humble himself more than ever before Him. This is the blessing that God desires that we, too, may receive whenever He permits Satan to strike us with sickness, and this end is attained by all sufferers who abandon themselves unreservedly to Him.

How are we to be delivered from sickness? A father never prolongs the chastisement of his child beyond the time necessary. God, also, who has His purpose in permitting sickness, will not prolong the chastisement longer than is necessary to attain His end. As soon as Job had understood Him, from the time that he condemned himself and repented in dust and ashes, through paying attention to what God had revealed to him of Himself, the chastisement was at an end. God Himself delivered Job from Satan's hand and healed him of his sickness.

If only the sick in our day understood that God has a distinct purpose in permitting their chastisement, and that as soon as it is attained—as soon as the Holy Spirit leads them to confess and forsake their sins and to consecrate themselves entirely to the service of the Lord—the chastisement will no longer be needed. The Lord can and will deliver them! God makes use of Satan as a wise government makes use of a jailer. He leaves His children in his power for the given time only. After that, His good will is to associate us with Christ, who has conquered Satan, withdrawing us from his domination by bearing our sins and our sicknesses for us.

Twenty-nine

The Prayer of Faith

The prayer of faith shall save the sick,
and the Lord shall raise him up.
—James 5:15

The prayer of faith"! Only once does this expression occur in the Bible, and it relates to the healing of the sick. The church has adopted this expression but hardly ever uses the prayer of faith, except to obtain other graces. According to Scripture, it is especially intended for the healing of the sick.

Did the apostle expect healing through the prayer of faith alone, or should it be accompanied by the use of remedies? This is generally the question that is raised. It is easily decided, if we take into consideration the power of the church's spiritual life in the early ages. This includes the gifts of healing bestowed on the apostles by the Lord, and augmented by the subsequent outpouring of the Holy Spirit (Acts 4:30; 5:15–16). What Paul said of *"these gifts of healing by the same Spirit"* (1 Cor. 12:9), James insisted on when he recalled Elijah's prayer and God's wonderful answer (James 5:17–18). All this clearly shows that the believer is to look for healing in response to the prayer of faith alone. Although God may use human remedies to aid in the healing, we must always remember that it is He who accomplishes the act.

Another question will arise: Does the use of remedies exclude the prayer of faith? To this, we believe our reply should be no, for the experience of a large number of believers testifies that, in answer to their prayers, God has often blessed the use of remedies and made them a means of healing.

We come here to a third question: What is the method to follow in order to prove with the greatest certainty, and according to the will of God, the effectiveness of the prayer of faith? Is it, according to James, in setting aside all remedies or in using remedies as believers do for the most part? In a word, is it with or without remedies that the prayer of faith best obtains the grace of God? Which of these two methods will be most directly to the glory of God and for blessing to the sick one? Is it not perfectly simple to reply that if the prescription and the promise in James apply to believers of our time, the blessing today will be just the same as it was then? It will apply to believers in all areas, if they expect healing by the direct intervention of the Lord Himself, without using any remedies. It is, in fact, in this sense that Scripture always speaks of powerful faith and of the prayer of faith.

Both the laws of nature and the witness of Scripture show us that God often makes use of intermediary agencies to manifest His glory. Under the power of the Fall and the control of our senses, our tendency is to attach more importance to the remedies than to the direct action of God. It often happens that we are so preoccupied with the remedies that we turn away from God. Thus the laws and the properties of nature, which were destined to bring us back to God, have the contrary effect.

This is why, when the Lord called Abraham to be the father of His chosen people, He did not follow the laws of nature (Rom. 4:17–21). God desired to form for Himself a people of faith, who lived more in the unseen than in the tangible world. In order to lead them into this life, it was necessary to take away their confidence in ordinary means. We see, therefore, that it was not by natural ways that God led Abraham, Jacob, Moses, Joshua, Gideon, the Judges, David, and many other kings of Israel. His objective was to teach them by this to confide only in Him, to know Him as He is: *"Thou art the God that doest wonders"* (Ps. 77:14).

God wills to act in a similar way with us. When we seek to walk according to His prescription in James 5, abandoning the *"things which are seen"* (2 Cor. 4:18) to grasp God's promise—the desired healing—directly from Him, we discover how much importance we have attached to earthly remedies. Undoubtedly, there are Christians who can make use of remedies without damage to their spiritual lives, but the larger number of them are apt to count much more on the remedies than on the power of God. God's desire is to lead His children into a more intimate communion with Christ, and this is just what does happen, when, by faith, we commit ourselves to Him as our sovereign Healer. When one is led by God to renounce remedies, his faith my be strengthened in an extraordinary manner. Healing then becomes a source of innumerable spiritual blessings. What faith can accomplish becomes more real to us. A new tie is established between God and the believer, commencing in him a life of confidence and dependence. The body and the soul are placed equally under the power of the Holy Spirit. Thus, the prayer of faith, which saves the sick, leads us to a life of faith, strengthened by the assurance that God manifests His presence in our earthly lives.

Thirty

Anointing in the Name of the Lord

Is any sick among you? let him call for the elders of the
church; and let them pray over him, anointing him with oil
in the name of the Lord.
—James 5:14

James' instructions to anoint the sick person with oil in the name of the Lord have given rise to controversy. Some have sought to infer that James had mentioned anointing with oil as a remedy to be employed, and that to anoint in the name of the Lord simply meant to rub the patient with oil. But since this prescription is made for all kinds of sickness, oil would have to possess a miraculous healing power. Let us see what the Scriptures tell us about anointing with oil, and what sense it attaches to the two words, *anointing* and *oil*.

It was the custom of the people in the East to anoint themselves with oil when they came out of the bath; it was most refreshing in a hot climate. We see, also, that all those who were called to the special service of God were to be anointed with oil, as a token of their consecration to God, and of the grace that they would receive from Him to fulfill their vocation. Thus the oil that was used to anoint the priests and the tabernacle was looked upon as *"most holy"* (Exod. 30:29). Wherever the Bible speaks of anointing with oil, it is an emblem of holiness and consecration. Nowhere in the Bible do we find any proof that oil was used as a medicine.

Anointing with oil is mentioned once in connection with sickness, but its place there was evidently as a religious ceremony and not as a medicine. In Mark 6:13, we read that the twelve *"cast out many devils, and anointed with oil many that were sick, and healed them."* Here the healing of the sick runs parallel with the casting out of devils: both are the result of miraculous power. Such was the kind of mission that Jesus commanded His disciples when He sent them two by two: *"He gave them power against unclean spirits, to cast them out, and to heal all manner of sickness and all manner of disease"* (Matt. 10:1). Thus, it was the same power that permitted them either to cast out devils or to heal the sick.

But let us seek to discover what was symbolized by the anointing administered by the twelve. In the Old Testament, oil was the symbol of the gift of the Holy Spirit: *"The Spirit of the Lord GOD is upon me; because the LORD hath anointed me"* (Isa. 61:1). It is said of the Lord Jesus in the New Testament, *"God anointed Jesus of Nazareth with the Holy Ghost and with power"* (Acts 10:38), and it is said of believers, *"Ye have an unction* [anointing] *from the Holy One"* (1 John 2:20). Sometimes man feels the need of a visible sign, appealing to his senses, that may come to his aid to sustain his faith and enable him to grasp the spiritual meaning. The anointing, therefore, should symbolize to the sick one the action of the Holy Spirit who gives the healing.

Do we then need the anointing as well as the prayer of faith? The Word of God prescribes it. In order to follow God's Word, most of those who pray for healing receive the anointing. This is not so much because they regard it as indispensable, but to show that they are ready to submit to the Word of God in all things. In the last promise made by the Lord Jesus, He ordains the laying on of hands, not the anointing, to accompany the communication of healing virtue (Mark 16:18). When Paul circumcised Timothy and took upon himself a special vow, it was to prove that he had no objection to observe the institutions of the old covenant as long as the liberty of the Gospel did not thereby suffer loss. In the same way, James, the head of the church of Jerusalem, faithful in preserving as far as possible the institutions of his fathers, continued the system of the Holy Spirit. And we also should regard it, not as a remedy, but as a pledge of the mighty virtue of the Holy Spirit, as a means of strengthening faith, a point of contact and of communion between the sick one and the members of the church who are called to anoint him with oil.

"I am the LORD that healeth thee" (Exod. 15:26).

Thirty-one

Full Salvation—Our High Privilege

Son, thou art ever with me, and all that I have is thine.
—Luke 15:31

We may talk a great deal about the father's love for the Prodigal Son, but when we think of the way he treated the elder brother, it brings to our hearts a truer sense of the wonderful love of the father.

I suppose that many readers of this book have "full salvation"; but perhaps more than half of you do not. You may not even understand the expression. Well, the great objective of this book is to bring you to see that full salvation is waiting for you now, and that God wants you to experience it. If you feel you do not have it, I wish to show you how wrong it is to be without it, and then to show you how to come out of that wrong life and into the right one. May all who do not have the experience pray very humbly, "Oh, my Father, bring me into the full enjoyment of Your full salvation."

In our parable, the elder son was always with his father and had two privileges: unceasing fellowship and unlimited partnership. But he was worse than the Prodigal Son, for, though he was always at home, he had never known, enjoyed, or understood these privileges. All this fullness of fellowship had been waiting for and offered to him, but he had not received it. While the Prodigal Son was away from home in the far country, his elder brother was far from the *enjoyment of* home, even while he was at home.

Full salvation includes unceasing fellowship: *"Ever with me."* An earthly father loves his child and delights to make his child happy. *"God is love"* (1 John 4:8), and He delights to pour out His own nature on His people. Many people talk about God hiding His face, but there are only two things that ever caused God to do so—sin and unbelief. Nothing else can. It is the very nature of the sun to shine, and it can't help shining on and on. *"God is love,"* and, speaking with all reverence, He can't help loving. We see His goodness toward the ungodly and His compassion on the erring. His fatherly love is manifested toward all His children.

"But," you say, "is it possible always to be happy and dwelling with God?" Yes, certainly, and there are many Scripture promises that speak to this point. Look at the epistle to the Hebrews, where we read of the *"boldness to enter into the holiest"* (Heb. 10:19). How often, too, did David speak of hiding *"in the secret of his tabernacle"* (Ps. 27:5) and dwelling *"under the shadow of the Almighty"* (Ps. 91:1)?

My message is that the Lord your God desires to have you living continually in the light of His countenance. Are your business, your temper, and your circumstances stronger than God? If you come and ask God to shine through them and onto you, you will see and prove that He can do it, and that you as a believer may walk all day long, every day, in the light of His love. That is "full salvation."

"Ever with Thee"; I never knew it, Lord, and so I did not enjoy it, but I do now.

Full salvation includes unlimited partnership: *"All that I have is thine."* The elder son complained of the father's gracious reception of the Prodigal—of all the feasting and rejoicing over his return—while he had never been given a lamb to enjoy in feasting with his friends. The father, in the tenderness of his love, answered him, "Son, you were always in my house; you had only to ask and you would have been given everything you desired and required." And that is what our Father says to all His children.

But you are saying, "I am so weak; I cannot conquer my sins; I can't manage to keep right; I can't do anything." No, you cannot, but God can. For so long, He has been saying to you, "All that I have is yours. I have given it to you in Christ. All the Spirit's power and wisdom, all the riches of Christ, all the love of the Father—there is nothing that I have that is not yours. I am God who will love, keep, and bless you."

Thus God speaks, but it seems all a dream to some. Why are you so poor? God's Word is sure, and does He not promise all this? In John 14–16, He tells us that we may have wonderful answers to prayer if we come in Jesus' name and abide in Him. Do we really believe that it is possible for a Christian to live such a life?

Now, we have looked at this great privilege, which is for everyone, so we move on to consider the poverty of many of God's dear children. It is nothing short of starvation. The elder son—the child of a rich man—living in utter poverty! He never had a fatted calf, while all that was his father's was his—just exactly the state of many a child of God! The way He wants us to live is in the fullest fellowship of all His blessings, yet what a contrast!

Ask some if their lives are full of joy; why, they don't even believe it is possible to be always happy and holy. "How could we survive like this in business?" they say, imagining the life of fullest blessing possible to be one of sighing and sadness and sorrow.

I asked a dear devoted Christian woman how she was doing. She answered that she experienced life as sometimes light and sometimes dark, arguing that, since this resembled nature, the kingdom of grace must be similar. So she willingly accepted a wretched experience. But I don't read in the Bible that there is to be any night or darkness in the believer's experience. On the contrary, I read, *"Thy sun shall no more go down"* (Isa. 60:20). Yet there are many who actually believe that there is nothing this good for them.

Again, nothing can hide God from us but sin and unbelief. If you are in spiritual poverty, with no joy and no experience of victory over sin, why is it so? You say, "I'm too weak; I must fall." But the Scriptures say that He is *"able to keep you from falling* [stumbling]*"* (Jude 24). A minister once told me that, although God is able, the verse does not say He is willing to do it. God does not mock us, beloved. If He says He is *"able,"* then it is a proof of His willingness to do it. Let us believe God's Word and examine our own experience in the light of it.

Again, are you working and bearing much fruit for God, and do people by your life see and say, "God is with that man, keeping him humble, pure, and heavenly minded"? Or are they forced to confess that you are just a very ordinary Christian, easily provoked, worldly, and not heavenly minded? That is not the life God wants us to live. We have a rich Father, and as no true earthly father would like to see his child in rags, or without shoes and proper clothing, neither does our God. He wishes to fill up our lives with the richest and choicest blessings.

How many Sunday school teachers there are who teach and teach, hoping for the conversion of their students, yet they can't say God uses them in the conversion of any of them. They enjoy no close fellowship with God, no victory over sin, no power to convince the world. To which class do you belong, the povertylevel or the fully saved? Confess it today.

These two sons represent two classes of Christians: the Prodigal, who is away and backslidden, and the elder son who is out of full fellowship with God. They were both poor. The elder son needed as great a change as the Prodigal. He needed to repent, confess, and claim his full privileges as a son. So should all low-level Christians repent, confess, and claim full salvation. Both of you, come today and say, "Father, I have sinned."

Now, ask why your experience is so much different than it should be. Ask yourself why you are not enjoying the full blessing. God's Word promises it, others speak of it, and some are actually living in it.

Oh, ask the reason. Come to God and say, "Why is it that I never live the life You want me to live?"

You will find the answer in our story. Just like the elder son, you have an unchildlike spirit and don't really know your Father. If you knew the real character of your Father, your life would be all right. You have, as it were, said, "I never got a calf to enjoy; my Father is rich, but He never gives. I have prayed quite enough, but God does not answer me. I hear other people say that God fills and satisfies them, but He never does that for me."

A dear minister once told me than an abundant life was not for everybody, that it was of God's sovereignty to give this to whomever He pleased.

Friends, there is no doubt as to God's sovereignty. He dispenses His gifts as He will. We are not all Pauls or Peters; places at the right and left hand of God are prepared for whomever He will. But this is not a matter of divine sovereignty; it is a question of a child's heritage. The Father's love offers to give to every child His full salvation in actual experience.

Now look at an earthly father. His children are of various ages, but all have equal right to the joy of their father's countenance. True, he gives to his son of twenty years more money than to the son of five, and he has more to speak of to the boy of fifteen than to the child of three. But his love toward them is all the same, and in their privileges as children, they are all alike. Likewise, God's love to His dear children is all the same.

Do not try to throw the blame on God, but say, "I have harbored bad thoughts about You, O God, and I have sinned. As a father, I have done for my children what I did not believe God was able and willing to do for me, and I have been lacking in childlike faith." Oh, believe in the love, the willingness, and the power of God to give you full salvation, and a change will surely come.

Now, let us consider the way of restoration, how to get out of this negative experience. The Prodigal Son repented, and so must those children of God who have been living within sight of, but not enjoying, His promises. Conversion is generally sudden, and a long repentance is usually a long impenitence.

Many in the church of Christ think it must take a long time to receive full salvation. Yes, it will take a long time if you do it yourself—indeed, you probably never will receive it.

But if you come and trust God, it can be done in a moment. By God's grace, give yourself up to Him. Don't say, "What's the use? It will do no good." Put yourself, just as you are, in sin and weakness, into the bosom of your Father. God will deliver you, and you will find that it is only one step out of the darkness into the light. Say, "Father, what a wretch I have been, to live with You and yet not believe Your love for me!"

I come today with a call to repent, addressed not to the unsaved, but to those who know what it is to be pardoned. Have you not sinned in the cold thoughts you have had of God, and is there not a longing, a thirsting, and a hungering after something better? Come, then; repent, and believe that God can simply blot out the sin of your unbelief. Do you believe it? Oh, do not dishonor God by unbelief, but come today and confidently claim full salvation. Then trust in Him to keep you. This seems difficult to some, but there is no difficulty about it. God will shine His light on you always, saying, *"Son, thou art ever with me."* All you have to do is dwell in and walk in that light.

I began by saying there are two classes of Christians: those who enjoy full salvation, and those who do not understand it. Well, if it is not clear to you, ask God to make it clear. But if you do understand it, remember, it is a definite act. Just let yourself go into the arms of God. Hear Him say, "Everything is yours." Then you will say, "Praise God, I believe, I accept, I give myself to Him, and I believe God gives Himself now to me!"

Thirty-two

"Ye Are the Branches"

Ye are the branches.
—John 15:5

What a simple thing it is to be a branch—the branch of a tree, or the branch of a vine! The branch grows out of the vine, or out of the tree, and there it lives and in due time bears fruit. It has no responsibility except receiving sap and nourishment from the root and stem.

If we only realized that our relationship to Jesus Christ, by way of the Holy Spirit, is like this! Our lives would become heavenly. Instead of soul-weariness or exhaustion, our work would be a new experience, linking us to Jesus as nothing else can.

Is it not often true that our work comes between us and Jesus? What folly it is to allow the very work He has to do in me, and I for Him, to separate me from Christ. Many a laborer has complained that he has too much work and not enough time for close communion with Jesus, that his usual work weakens his inclination for prayer, and that even spending too much time with people clouds his spiritual life. What a sad thought that the bearing of fruit should separate the branch from the vine! That must be because we have looked at our work as something other than the branch bearing fruit. May God deliver us from every false thought about the Christian life.

Now, just a few thoughts about this blessed branch-life:

In the first place, it is a life of absolute dependence. The branch has nothing; it depends on the vine for everything. That phrase, *absolute dependence,* is one of the most solemn and precious phrases. A great German theologian wrote two large volumes some years ago to show that the whole of Calvin's theology is summed up in that one principle of absolute dependence on God, and he was right. If you can learn every moment of the day to depend on God, everything will turn out right. You will get the higher life if you depend absolutely on God.

I must understand, when I have to work, when I have to preach a sermon, or when I have to address a Bible class or go out and visit the poor, that all the responsibility of the work is His. That is exactly what Christ wants you to understand. Christ desires that the very foundation of all your work should be this simple, blessed consciousness: Christ must care for everything.

And how does He fulfill the trust of that dependence? He does it by sending down the Holy Spirit, not only now and then as a special gift, but hourly, daily, unceasingly, the living connection between the vine and the branches is maintained. The sap does not flow for a time, then stop, and then flow again. Rather, from moment to moment the sap flows from the vine to the branches. And just like this, my Lord Jesus wants me to take that blessed position as His worker. Morning by morning, day by day, hour by hour, and step by step, I must abide in Him in the simple, utter helplessness of one who knows nothing, and is nothing, and can do nothing.

Absolute dependence on God is the secret of all power in work. The branch has nothing but what it gets from the vine, and you and I can have nothing but what we get from Jesus.

The life of the branch is not only a life of entire dependence, but of deep restfulness. If that little branch could talk to us, we could ask it, "Branch of the vine, how can I be a true branch of the living Vine?" The little branch would answer, "I hear that you are wise, and I know that you can do a great many wonderful things. You have much strength and wisdom given to you, but I have one lesson for you. With all your hurry and effort in Christ's work, you never prosper. The first thing you need is to come and rest in your Lord Jesus. That is what I do.

"Since I grew out of that vine, I have spent years and years doing nothing but resting in the vine. When spring came, I had no anxious thought or care. The vine began to pour its sap into me, and produced the bud and leaf. When the summer came, I had no care, trusting the vine to bring moisture to keep me fresh in the great heat. At harvest time, when the owner came to pluck the grapes, I had no care. If the grapes were not good, the owner never blamed the branch; the blame was always on the vine. If you desire to be a true branch of Christ, the living Vine, just rest on Him. Let Christ bear the responsibility."

You say, "Won't that make me slothful?" I tell you it will not. No one who learns to rest on the living Christ can become slothful, for the closer your contact with Christ, the more the Spirit of His zeal and love will fill you. A man sometimes tries and tries to be dependent on Christ. But by worrying about this absolute dependence, he tries and he cannot get it. Instead of worrying, he should sink down into entire restfulness every day.

Rest in Christ, who can give wisdom and strength. That restfulness will often prove to be the very best part of your Christian witness. You can plead with people, and you can argue. All they will know is that a man is arguing and striving with them. This is what happens when two men deal with each other, without Christ. But if you will let the deep rest of God come over you—the rest in Christ Jesus, the peace and holiness of heaven—that restfulness will bring a blessing to your heart, even more than the words you speak.

Furthermore, the branch teaches a lesson of much fruitfulness. You know the Lord Jesus repeated the word *fruit* often in that parable; He spoke first of *fruit*, then of *more fruit,* finally of *much fruit.* Yes, you are ordained not only to bear fruit, but also to bear much fruit. *"Herein is my Father glorified, that ye bear much fruit"* (John 15:8). In the first place, Christ said, "I am the Vine, and My Father is the Husbandman who has charge of Me and you." He who will watch over the connection between Christ and the branches is God; and it is in the power of God, through Christ, that we are to bear fruit.

O Christians, this world is perishing because of the lack of workers! And it needs more than workers. Some are saying, "We need not only more workers, but also workers with a new power, a different life, so that the workers will be able to bring more blessing."

What is missing is the close connection between the worker and the heavenly Vine. Christ, the heavenly Vine, has blessings that He could pour on tens of thousands who are perishing. Christ, the heavenly Vine, has the power to provide heavenly grapes. But *"ye are the branches,"* and you cannot bear heavenly fruit unless you are in close connection with Jesus Christ.

Do not confuse work and fruit. There is a good deal of work for Christ that is not the fruit of the heavenly Vine. Do not seek work only. Study this question of fruit-bearing. It is the very life, power, Spirit, and love within the heart of the Son of God; it means the heavenly Vine Himself coming into your heart and mine.

Stand in close connection with the heavenly Vine and say, "Lord Jesus, we ask for nothing less than the sap that flows through You, nothing less than the Spirit of Your divine life. Lord Jesus, let your Spirit flow through me in all my work for You."

Once again, the sap of the heavenly Vine is nothing but the Holy Spirit, and the Holy Spirit is nothing but the life of the heavenly Vine. What you must get from Christ is nothing less than a strong inflow of the Holy Spirit. You need it exceedingly, and you need nothing more. Remember this. Do not expect Christ to give a bit of strength here, a bit of blessing yonder, and a bit of help over there. As the vine does its work in giving its own unique sap to the branch, expect Christ to give His own Holy Spirit to your heart. Then you will bear much fruit. And if you have only begun to bear fruit and are listening to the words of Christ in the parable, *"more fruit,"* *"much fruit,"* remember that in order for you to bear more fruit, you just require more of Jesus in your life and heart.

Keep in mind that the life of the branch is a life of close communion. Such communion can be described only by Christ's precious inexhaustible word: *abiding.* Your life is to be an abiding life. Just like the branch in the vine, abide every minute of the day. The branches are in close communion—in unbroken communion—with the vine, from January to December.

You say you are too busy with other things. You may do ten hours of hard work daily, during which your brain has to be occupied with temporal things; God orders it so. But the abiding work is the work of the heart, not of the brain. It is the work of the heart clinging to and resting in Jesus, a work in which the Holy Spirit links us to Christ Jesus. Oh, believe that deeper down than the brain—deep down in the inner life—you can abide in Christ. Then every moment you are free, the awareness will come: "Blessed Jesus, I am still in You." If you will learn for a time to put aside other work and to get into this abiding contact with the heavenly Vine, you will find that fruit will come.

What is the application of this abiding communion to our everyday life? What does it mean? It means close fellowship with Christ in secret prayer. Many Christians have experienced a great inflow of

heavenly joy and a great outflow of heavenly gladness
that has, after a time, passed away. They have not
understood that close, personal, actual communion
with Christ is an absolute necessity for daily life.
Take time to be alone with Christ. Nothing in
heaven or earth can free you from the necessity for
that, if you are to be happy and holy Christians.

How many Christians look at it as a burden, a
duty, and a difficulty to be alone with God! That is
the great hindrance to our Christian life everywhere.

We need more quiet fellowship with God. You
cannot be healthy branches—branches into which
the heavenly sap can flow—unless you take plenty of
time for communion with God. If you are not willing
to sacrifice time to be alone with Him, giving Him
time every day to work in you and to maintain the
connection between you and Himself, He cannot give
you that blessing of His unbroken fellowship. Jesus
Christ asks you to live in close communion with
Him. Let every heart say, "O Christ, it is this I long
for; it is this I choose." And He will gladly give it to
you.

The life of the branch is a life of entire surrender. *Entire surrender* is a great and solemn concept
that is difficult to understand, yet the little branch
preaches it. "Can you do anything, little branch, besides bearing grapes?" "No, nothing." "Are you fit
for nothing?" "Fit for nothing!" The Bible says that
a bit of vine cannot even be used as a pen; it is fit for
nothing but to be burned. "And now, little branch,
what do you understand about your relationship to
the vine?" "My relationship is just this: I am entirely
given up to the vine; it can give me as much or as

little sap as it chooses. I am at its disposal, and the vine can do with me what it likes."

We need this entire surrender to the Lord Jesus Christ. One of the most difficult points to make clear, and one of the most important and necessary points to explain, is what this entire surrender is. It is an easy thing for a man or a number of men to offer themselves up to God for entire consecration, and to say, "Lord, it is my desire to give myself entirely to You." That is of great value, and often brings a very rich blessing. But the one question that should be studied quietly is, What is meant by entire surrender?

It means that, just as literally as Christ was given up entirely to God, I am given up entirely to Christ. Some think that it is too strong. Some think it can never be. But it is true. Just as completely as Christ gave up His life to do nothing but seek the Father's pleasure, depending on the Father absolutely, I am to do nothing but seek the pleasure of Christ.

Christ Jesus came to breathe His own Spirit into us, to make us find our very highest happiness in living entirely for God, just as He did. Fellow believers, if that is the case, then I ought to say, "Yes, as true as it is of that little branch of the vine, so by God's grace, I would have it be true of me. I desire to live day by day, allowing Christ to do with me what He will."

Here lies the terrible mistake of so much of our own religion. A man thinks, "I have my business, my family duties, and my responsibilities as a citizen, all of which I cannot change. Now, in addition to all of this, I am to enlist in the service of God as something

that will keep me from sin. May He help me to per-
form my duties properly!"

That is not right. When Christ came, He came
and bought the sinner with His blood. If there were a
slave market here and I were to buy a slave, I would
take that slave away from his old surroundings, and
he would live at my house as my personal property,
where I could order him about all day long. If he
were a faithful slave, he would live as having no will
and no interests of his own, his one care being to
promote the well-being and honor of his master. In
like manner, I, who have been bought with the blood
of Christ, have been bought to live every day with
only one thought: How can I please my Master?

We find the Christian life so difficult because we
seek God's blessing while we live in our own wills.
We would much rather live the Christian life according to our own liking. We could make our own
plans and choose our own work. Then we ask the
Lord Jesus to come in and guard us against sin and
see that we do not go too far wrong. We also ask Him
for much of His blessing.

But our relationship to Jesus ought to be such
that we are entirely at His disposal. Every day we
should go to Him humbly and straightforwardly and
say, "Lord, is there anything in me that is not according to Your will, that has not been ordered by
You, or that is not entirely given up to You?" If we
could then wait patiently, a relationship would
spring up between us that was so close and so ten-
der, we would be amazed at the distance in our previous relationship.

There are a great many difficulties with the
question of holiness, and much disagreement about

it. If only everyone could honestly long to be free from every sin. But our hearts often compromise with the idea: "We cannot be without sin; we must sin a little every day; we cannot help it." Instead, we must actually cry to God, "Lord, keep me from sin!" Give yourself utterly to Jesus, and ask Him to do His utmost for you in keeping you from sin.

In conclusion, let me gather everything together. Christ Jesus said, *"I am the vine, ye are the branches"* (John 15:5). In other words: "I, the living One who has so completely given Myself to you, am the Vine. You cannot trust Me too much. I am the almighty Worker, full of divine life and power."

Christians, you are the branches of the Lord Jesus Christ. Your heart may lack the consciousness of being a strong, healthy, fruit-bearing branch, closely linked with Jesus. If you are not living in Him as you should be, then listen to Him saying, "I am the Vine. I will receive you, and I will draw you to Myself. I will bless you and strengthen you. I will fill you with My Spirit. I, the Vine, have taken you to be My branches. I have given Myself utterly to you; children, give yourselves utterly to Me. I have surrendered Myself as God absolutely to you. I became Man and died for you so that I might be entirely yours. Come and surrender yourselves entirely to be Mine."

What will our answer be? Oh, let it be a prayer from the depths of our hearts, that the living Christ may take each one of us and link us closely to Himself. Let our prayer be that He, the living Vine, will link each of us to Himself in such a way that we will walk victoriously, with our hearts singing, "He is my Vine, and I am His branch. I want nothing more, now that I have the everlasting Vine." Then, when you get alone with Him, worship and adore Him, praise and trust Him, love Him and wait for His love. "You are my Vine, and I am Your branch. It is enough; my soul is satisfied. Glory to His blessed name!"

About the Author

A ndrew Murray (1828–1917) was born to a godly Scottish couple who had emigrated to South Africa. After being educated in Scotland and Holland, Andrew Murray returned to his beloved adopted country. He was ordained in the Dutch Reformed Church and assigned to a pastorate in a remote area of South Africa. His parish covered an area about the size of North Carolina. His parishioners, made up of farmers and ranchers, were scattered great distances from one another. Perhaps, as a result, Andrew Murray became an amazingly prolific Christian writer as his books became an extension of his pastoral work.

Some of Murray's earliest works were written to provide nurture and guidance to Christians, whether young or old in the faith. Once books such as *Abide in Christ, Like Christ,* and *With Christ in the School of Prayer* were written, Murray became widely known, and new books from his pen were awaited with great eagerness throughout the world.

Writing to many of the people in his congregation who could come into town for church services only on rare occasions, his books provided daily practical help for his readers' spiritual growth. As he wrote these books of instruction, Murray adopted the practice of placing many of his more devotional books into thirty-one separate readings to correspond with the days of the month.

At the age of seventy-eight, Murray resigned from the pastorate and devoted most of his time to his manuscripts. He continued to write profusely, moving from one book to the next with an intensity of purpose and a zeal that few men of God have ever equaled. He often said of himself, rather humorously, that he was like a hen about to hatch an egg; he was restless and unhappy until he got the burden of the message off his mind.

During these later years, after hearing of pocket-sized paperbacks, Andrew Murray immediately began to write books to be published in that fashion. He thought it was a splendid way to have the teachings of the Christian life at one's fingertips, where they could be carried around and read at any time of the day.

One source has said of Andrew Murray that his prolific style possesses the strength and eloquence that are born of deep earnestness and a sense of the solemnity of the issues of the Christian life. Nearly every page reveals an intensity of purpose and appeal that stirs men to the depths of their souls. Murray moves the emotions, searches the conscience, and reveals the sins and shortcomings of many of us with a love and hope born out of an intimate knowledge of the mercy and faithfulness of God.

For Andrew Murray, prayer was considered our personal home base from which we live our Christian lives and extend ourselves to others. During his later years, the vital necessity of unceasing prayer in the spiritual life came to the forefront of his teachings. It was then that he revealed the secret treasures of his heart concerning a life of persistent and believing prayer.

Countless persons the world over have hailed Andrew Murray as their spiritual father and given credit for much of their Christian growth to the influence of his priceless devotional books.

The condition of God's blessing is absolute surrender of all into His hands. If our hearts are willing for that, there is no end to what God will do for us, and to the blessings God will bestow.

—ANDREW MURRAY

ANOTHER POWERFUL Book

from Whitaker House

Prayer
Charles H. Spurgeon

If you struggle to find the words to praise God, to ask for His favor, or to claim all His benefits, join in prayer with Charles Spurgeon. His prayers were eloquent yet simple, and they'll take you straight to the merciful throne of God. You'll find healing, joy, forgiveness, and deeper fellowship with the Lord, and you'll be effective in prayer for others!

ISBN: 0-88368-562-0 Trade 192 pages

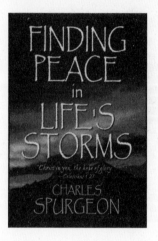